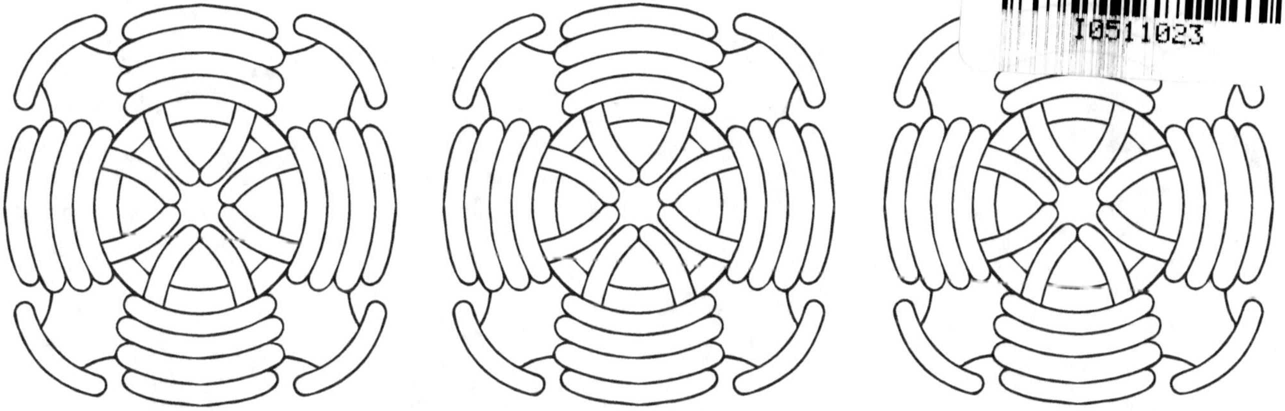

CALMING **PATTERNS**

Lori's Pattern Coloring Books for Adults

VOLUME 3

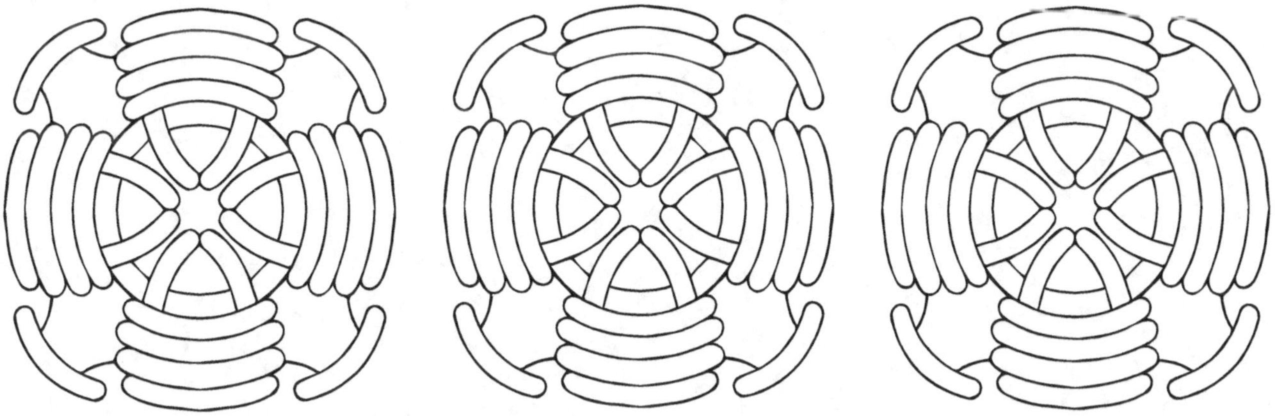

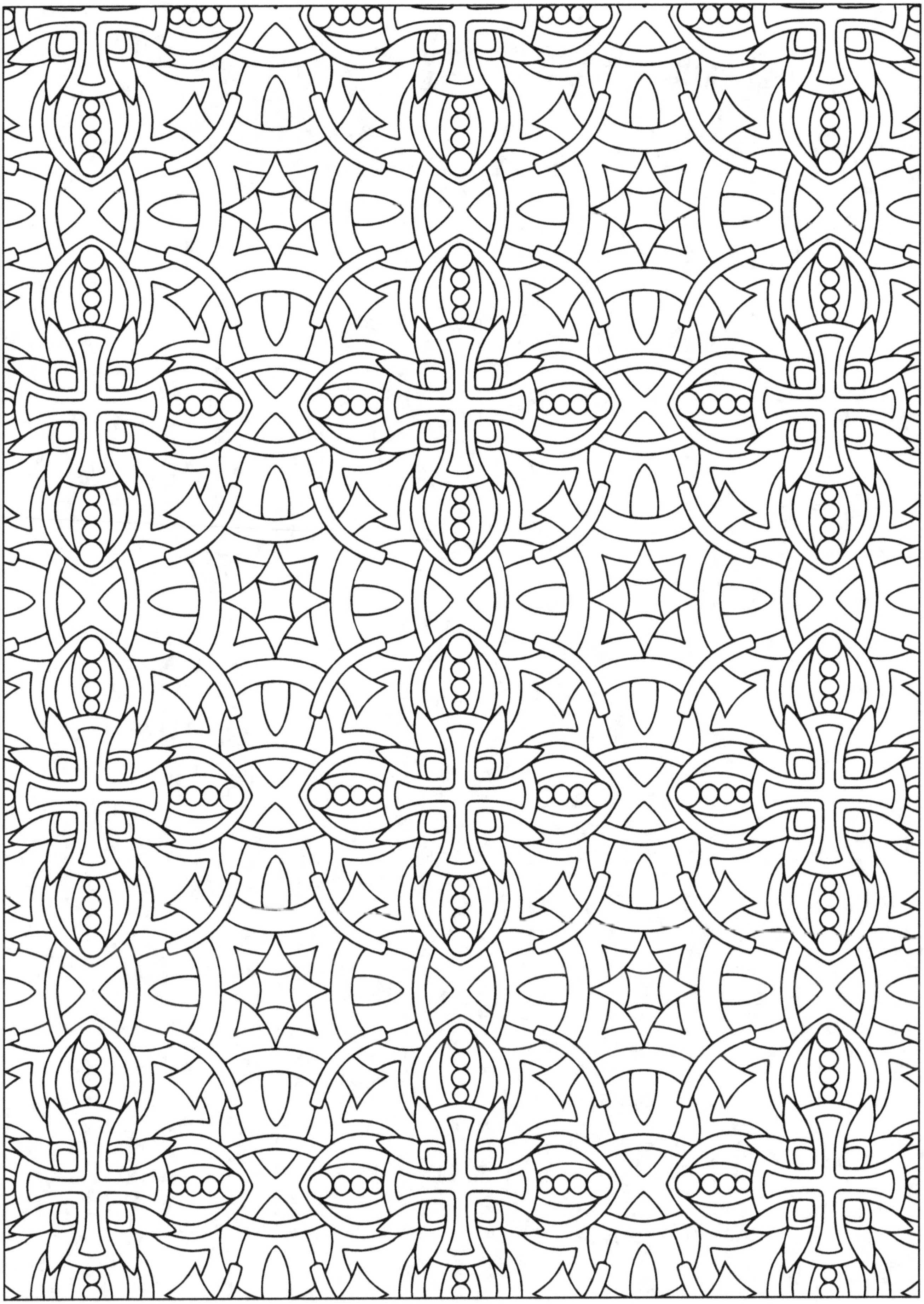

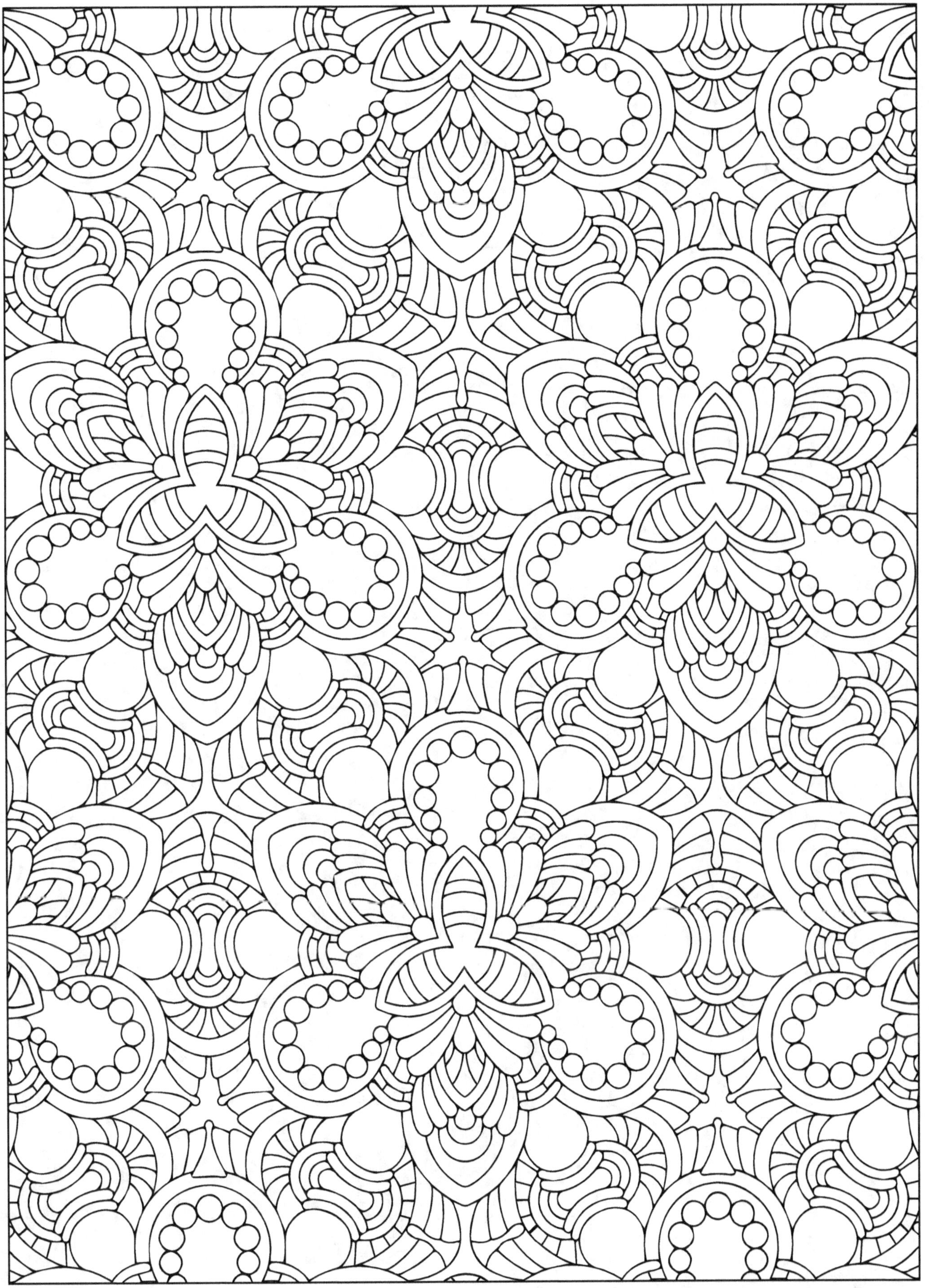

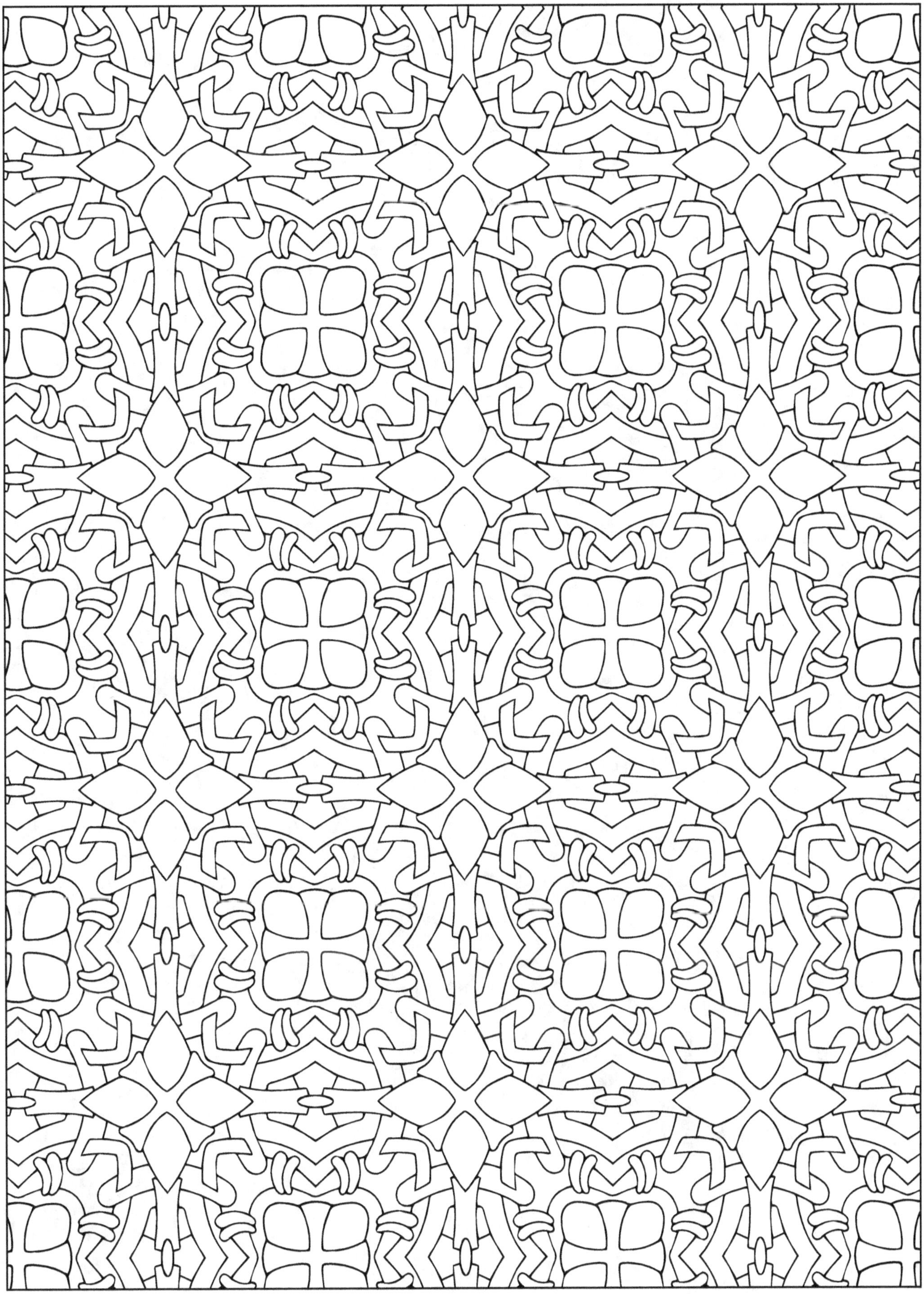

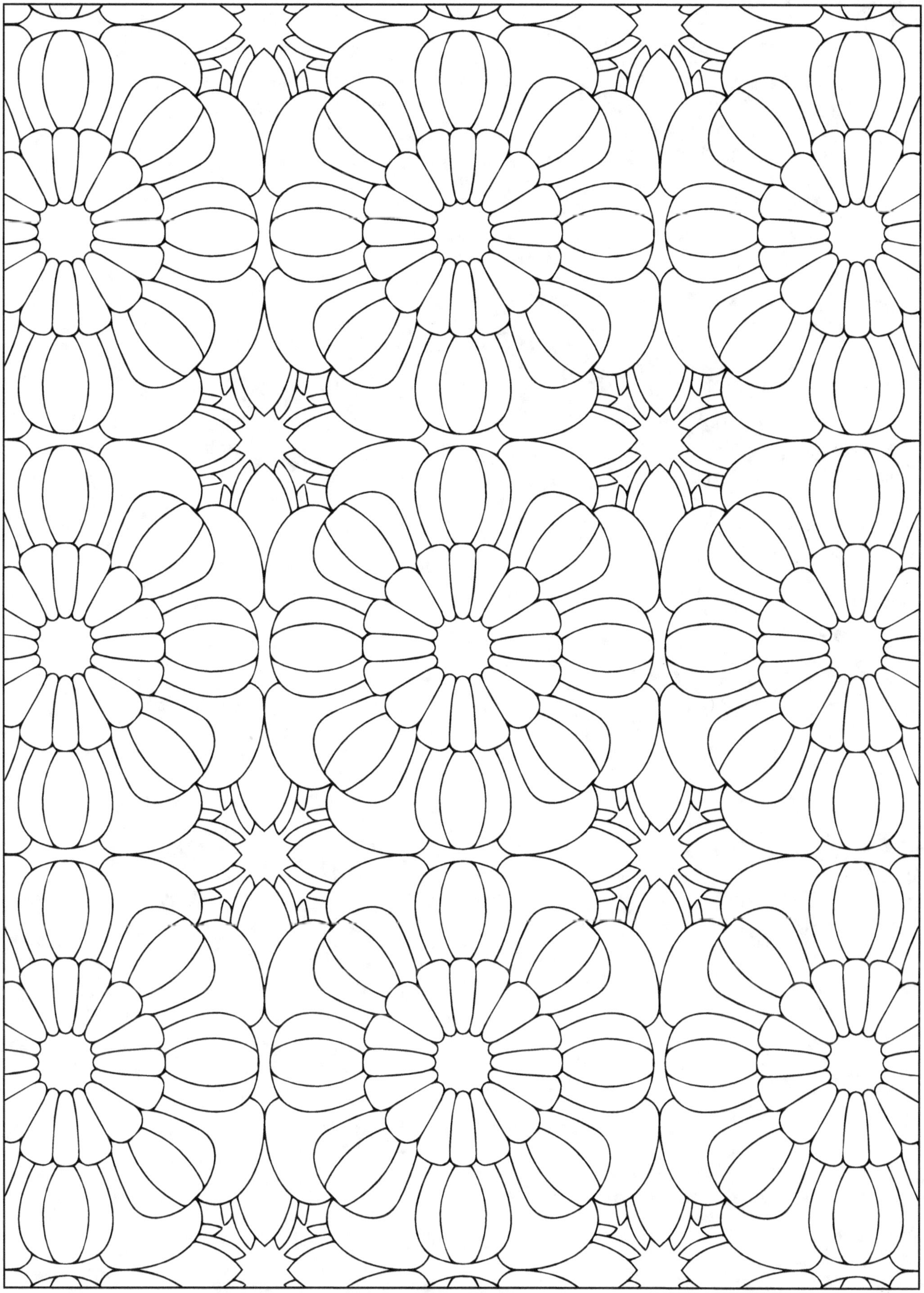

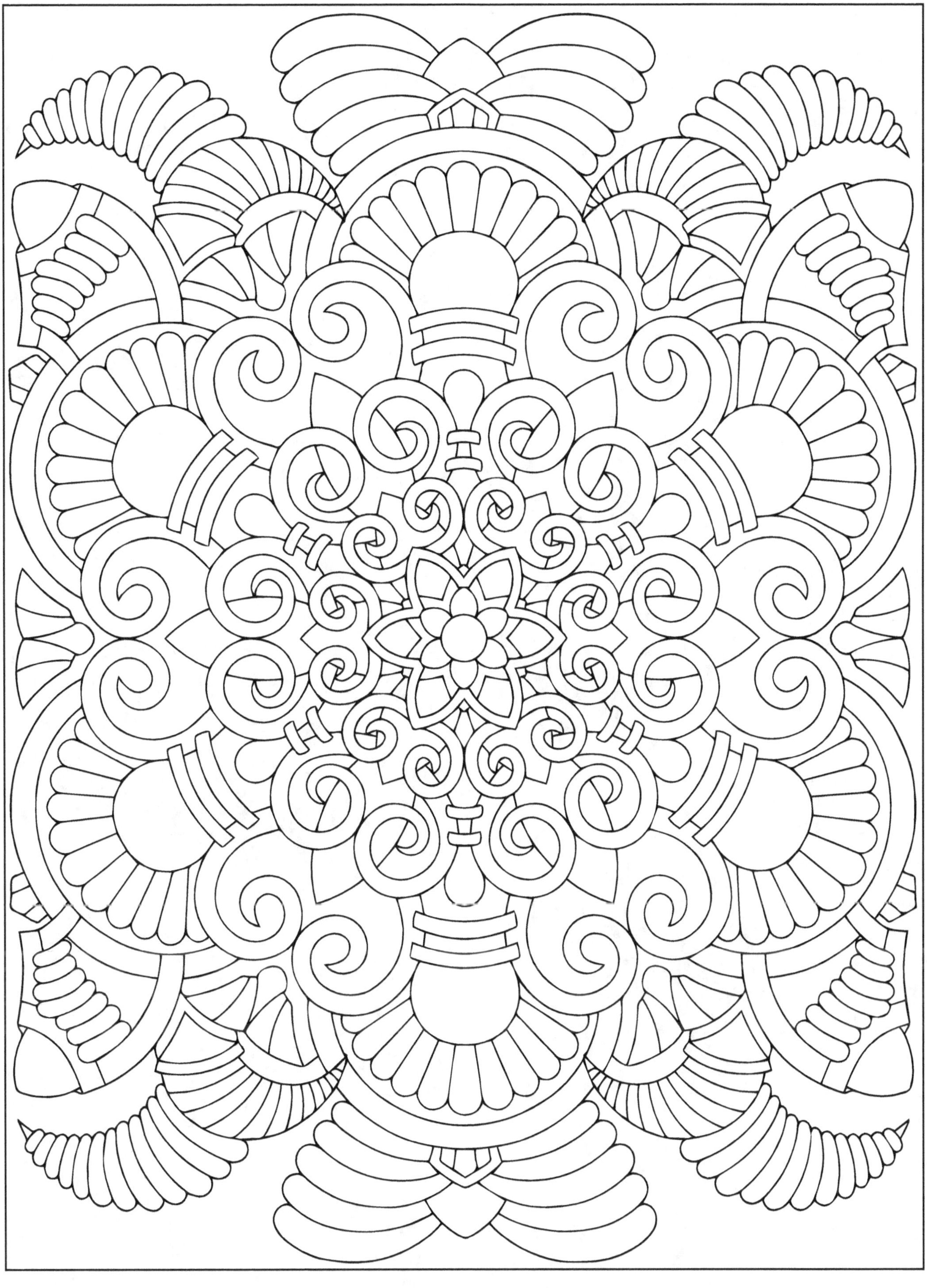

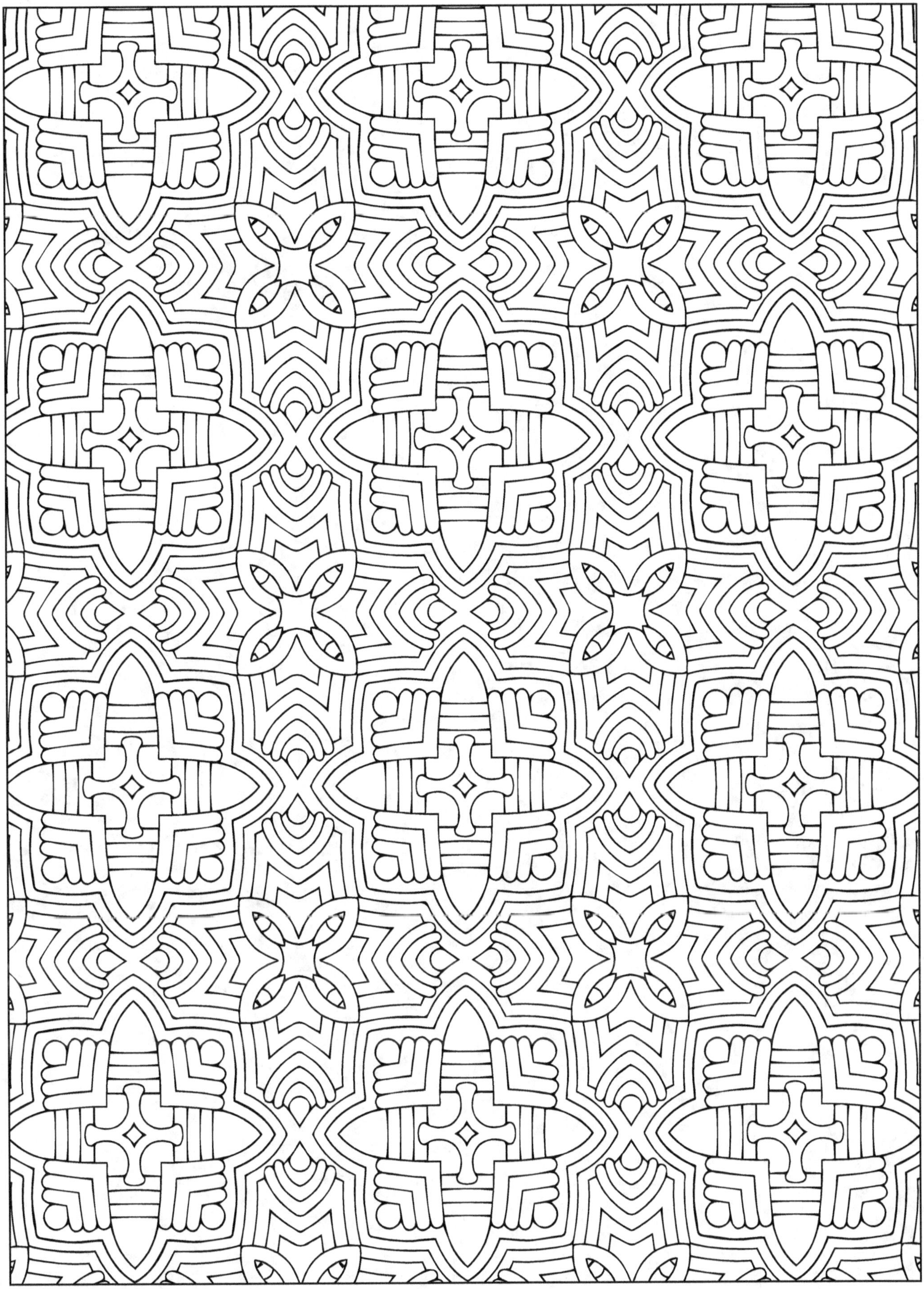

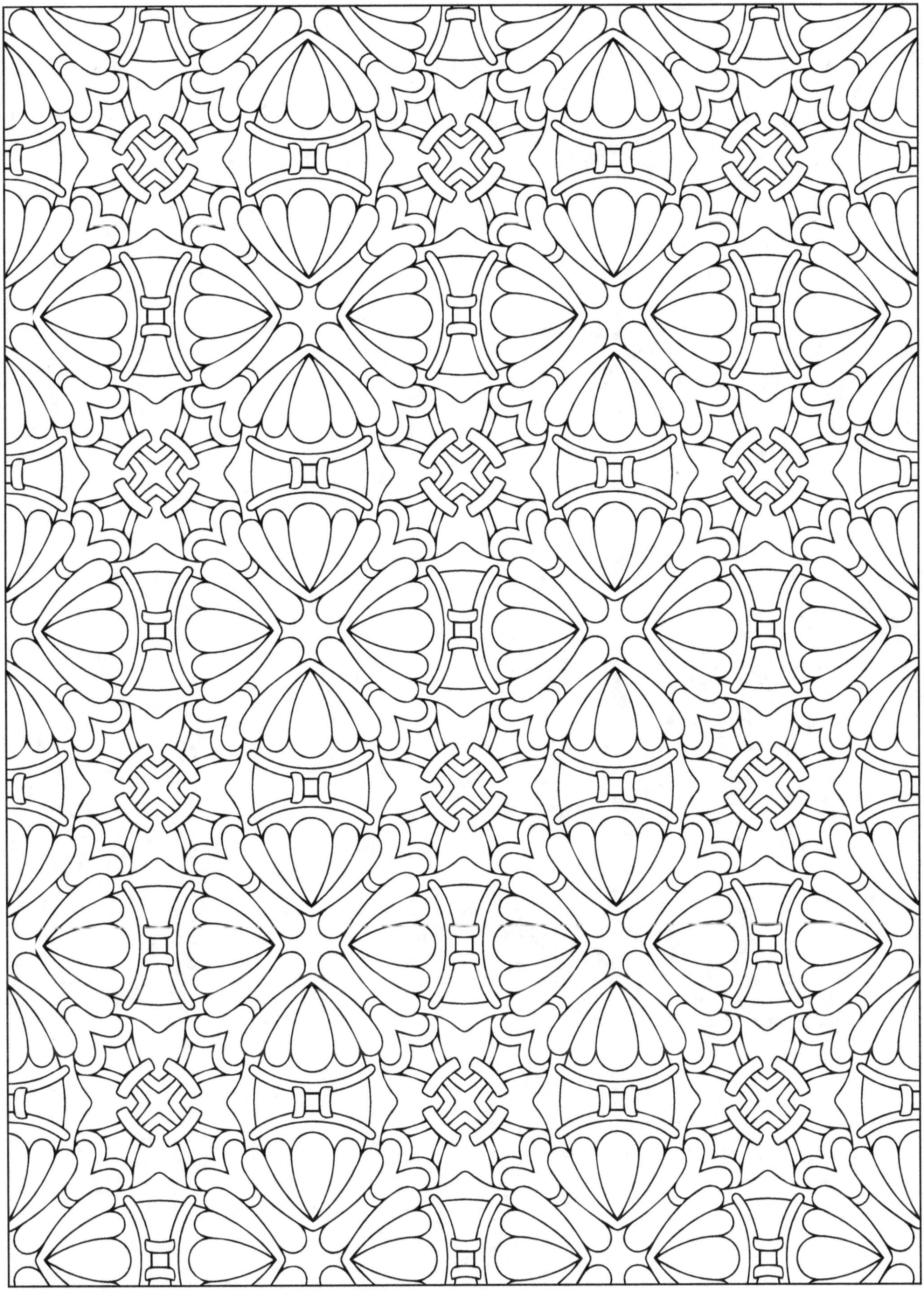

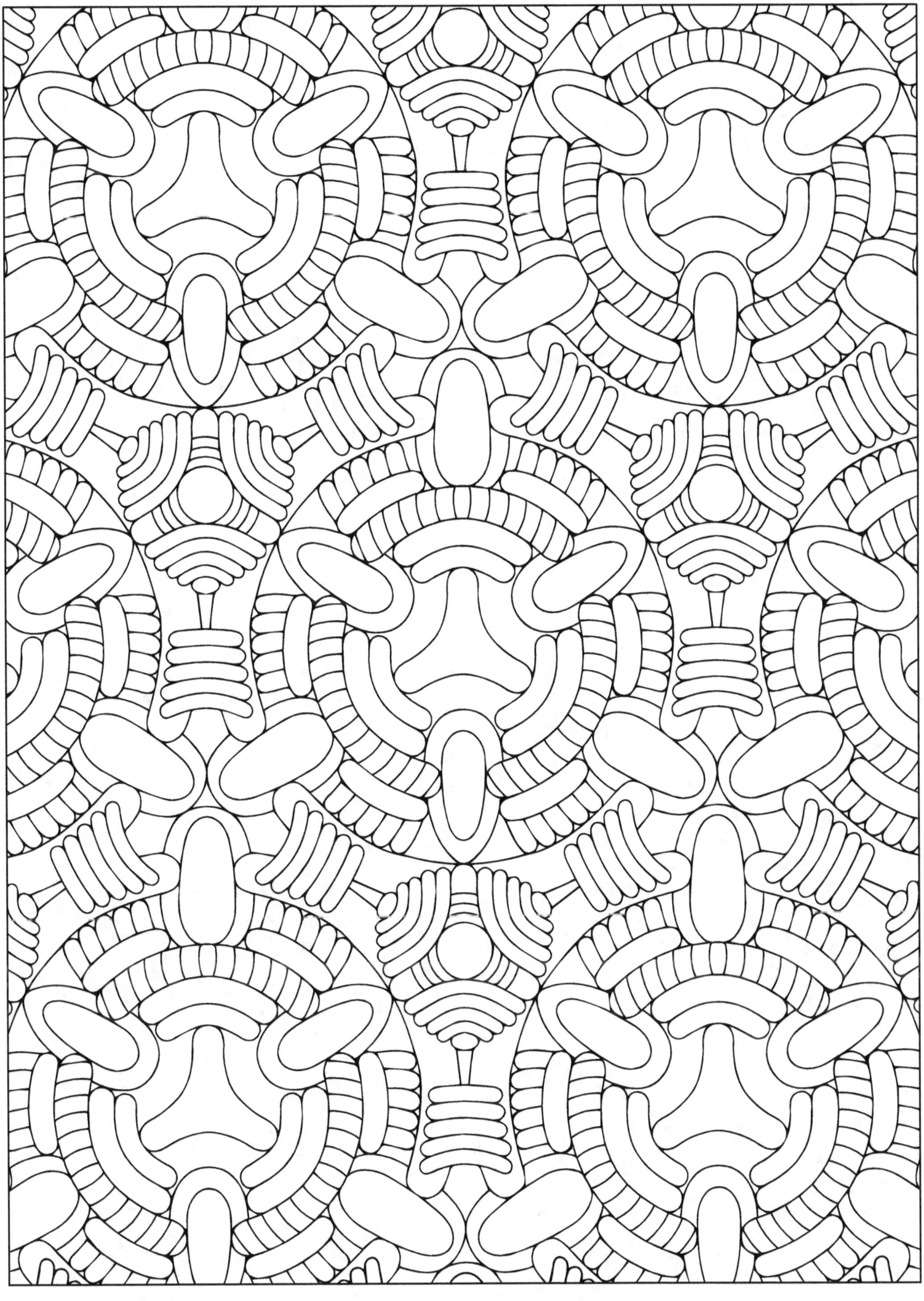

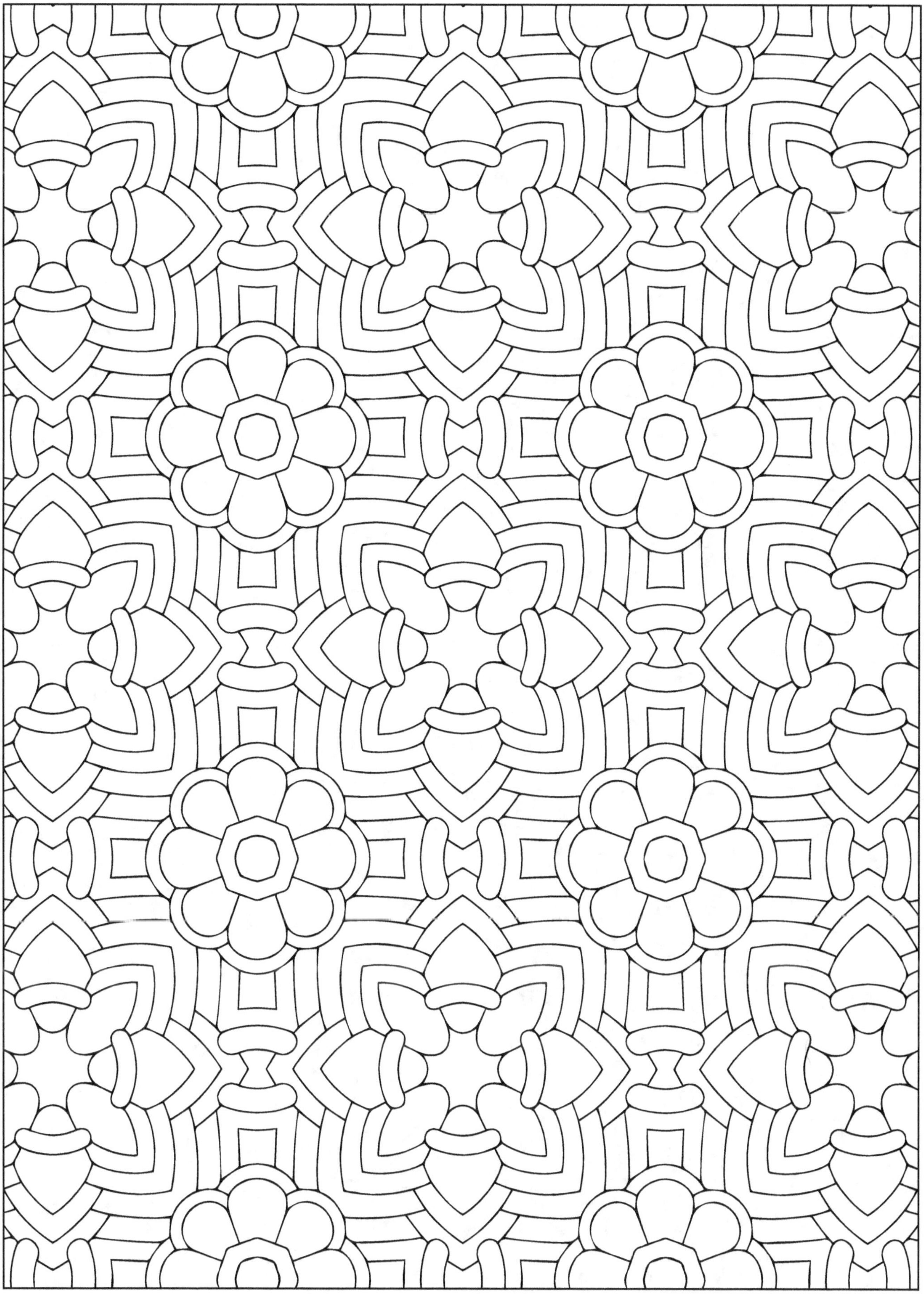

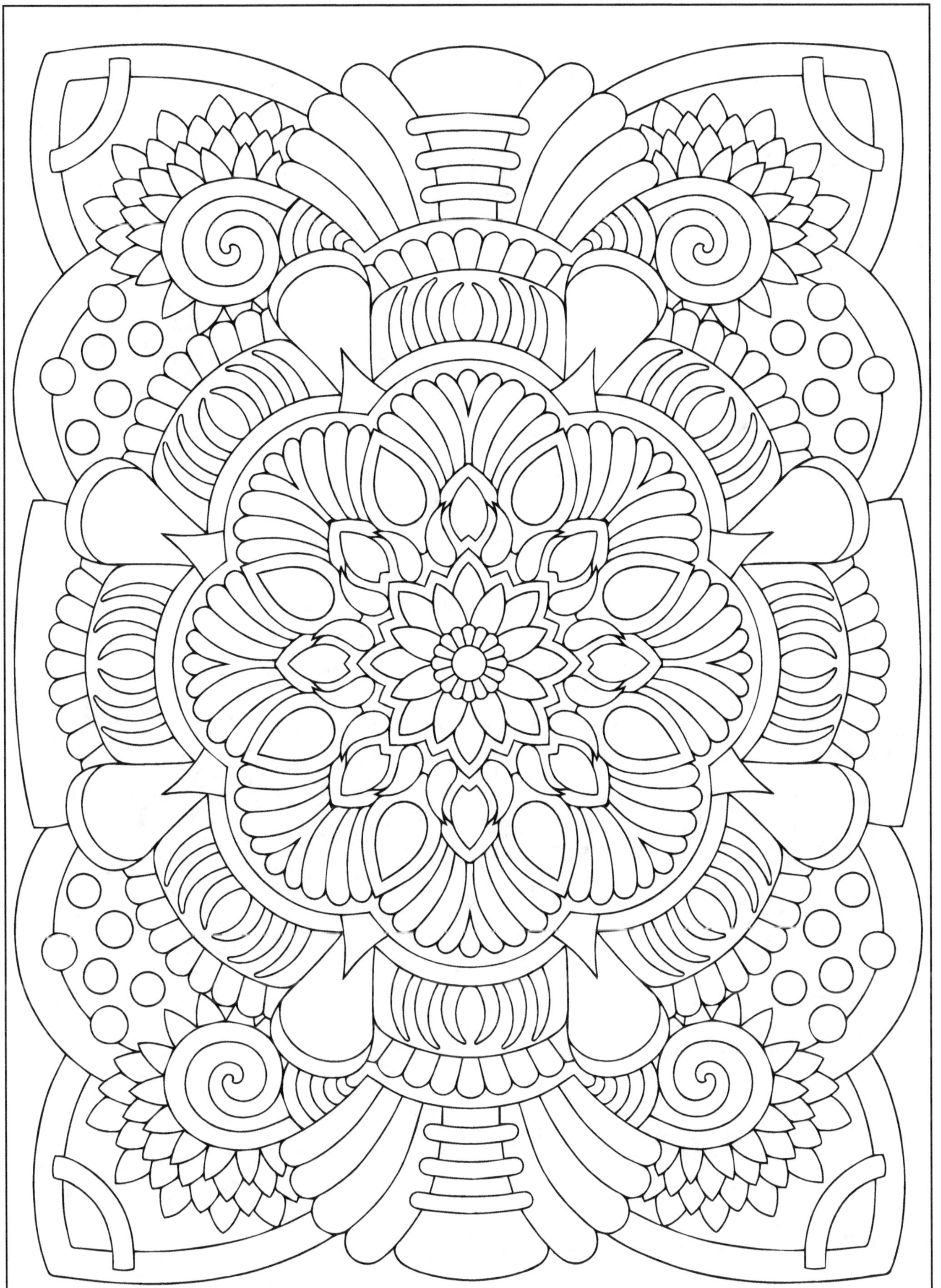

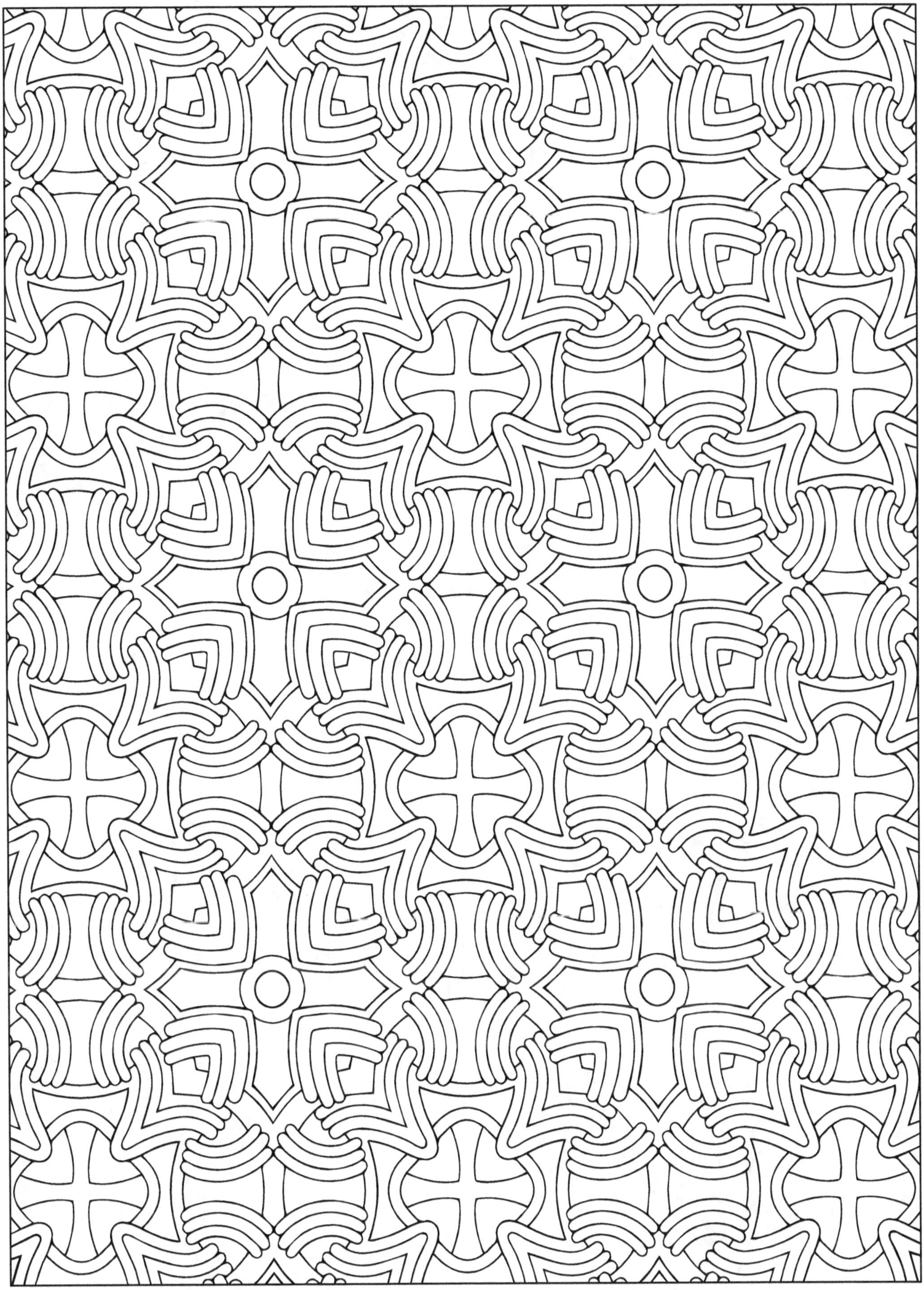

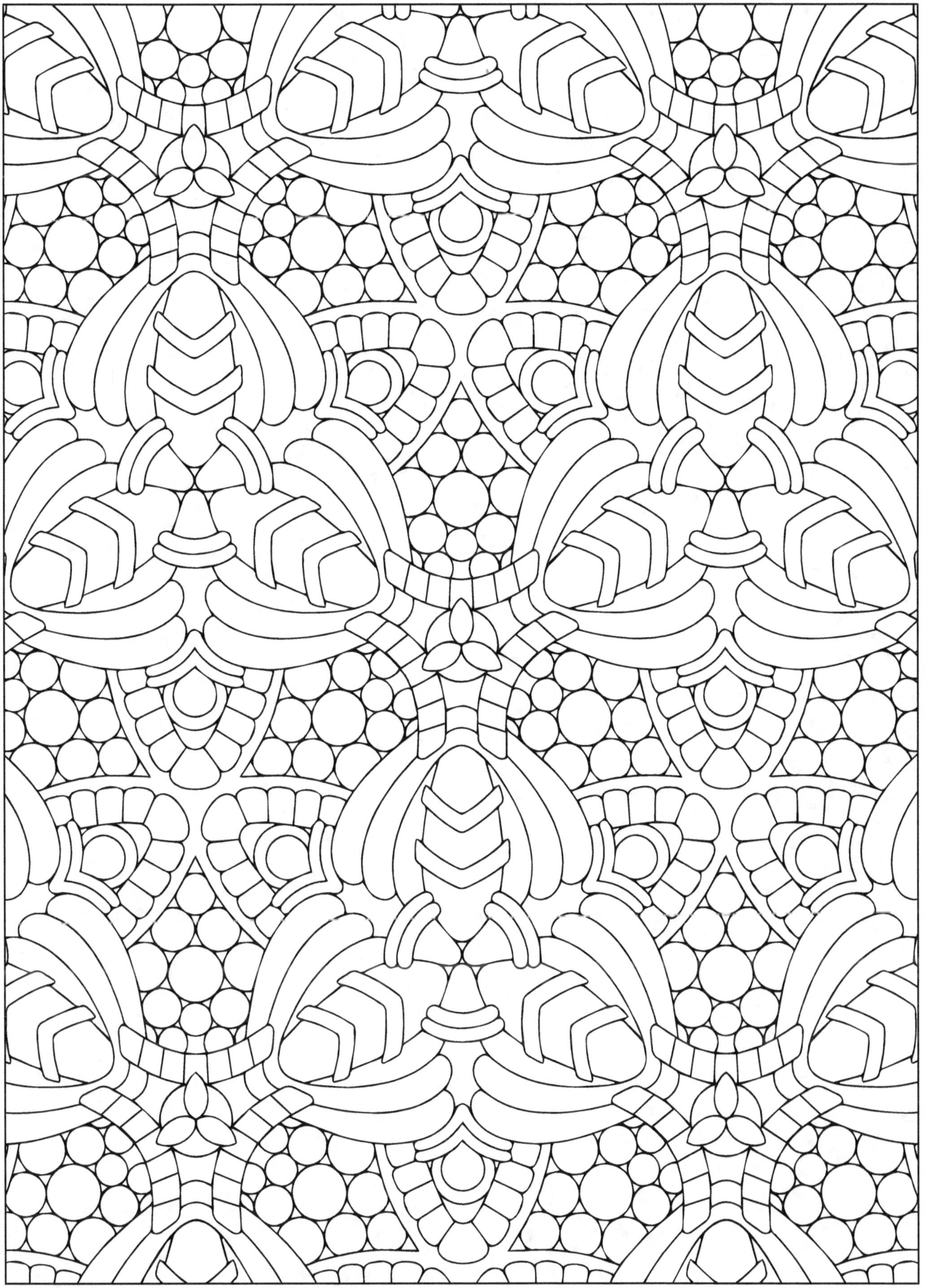

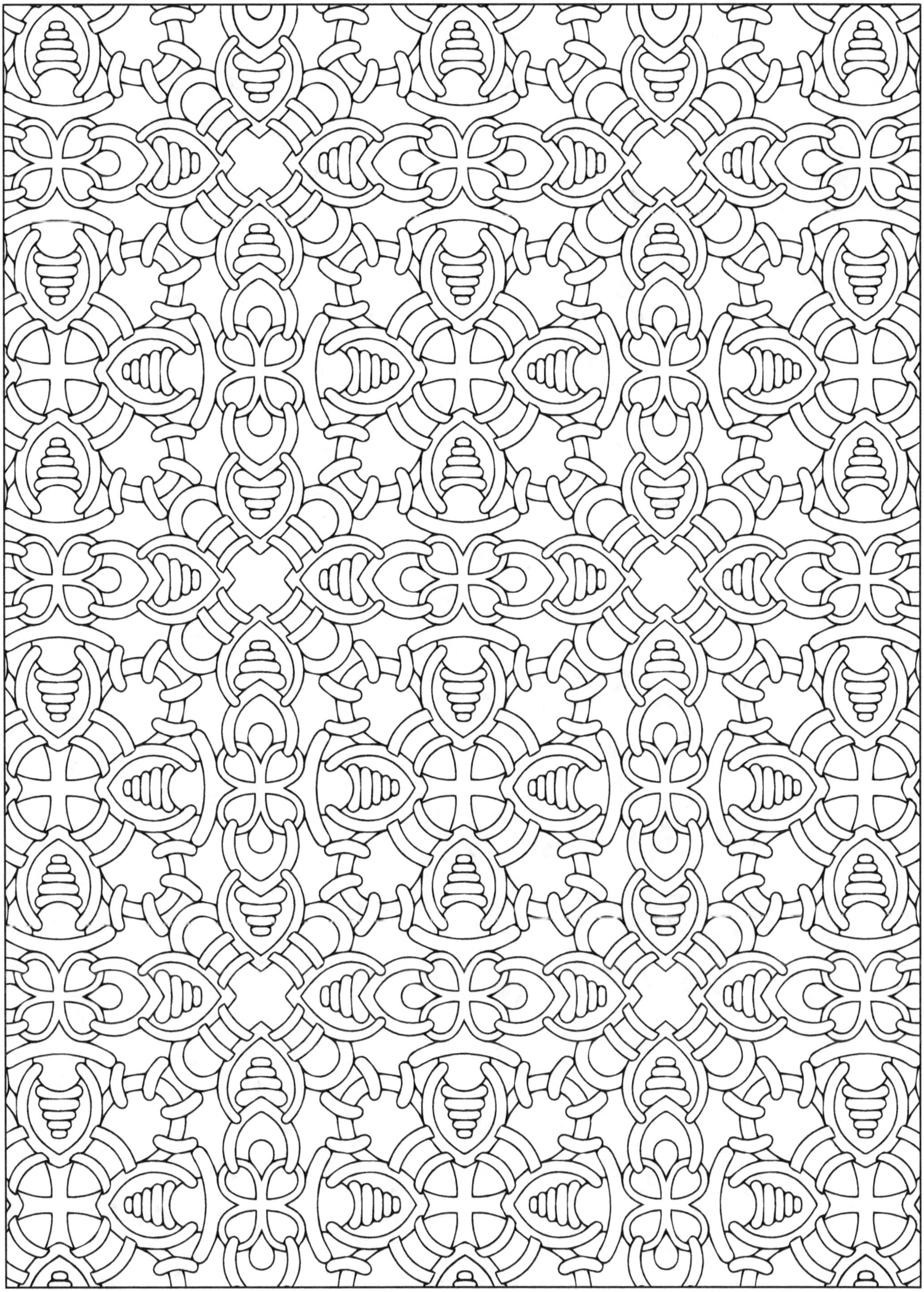

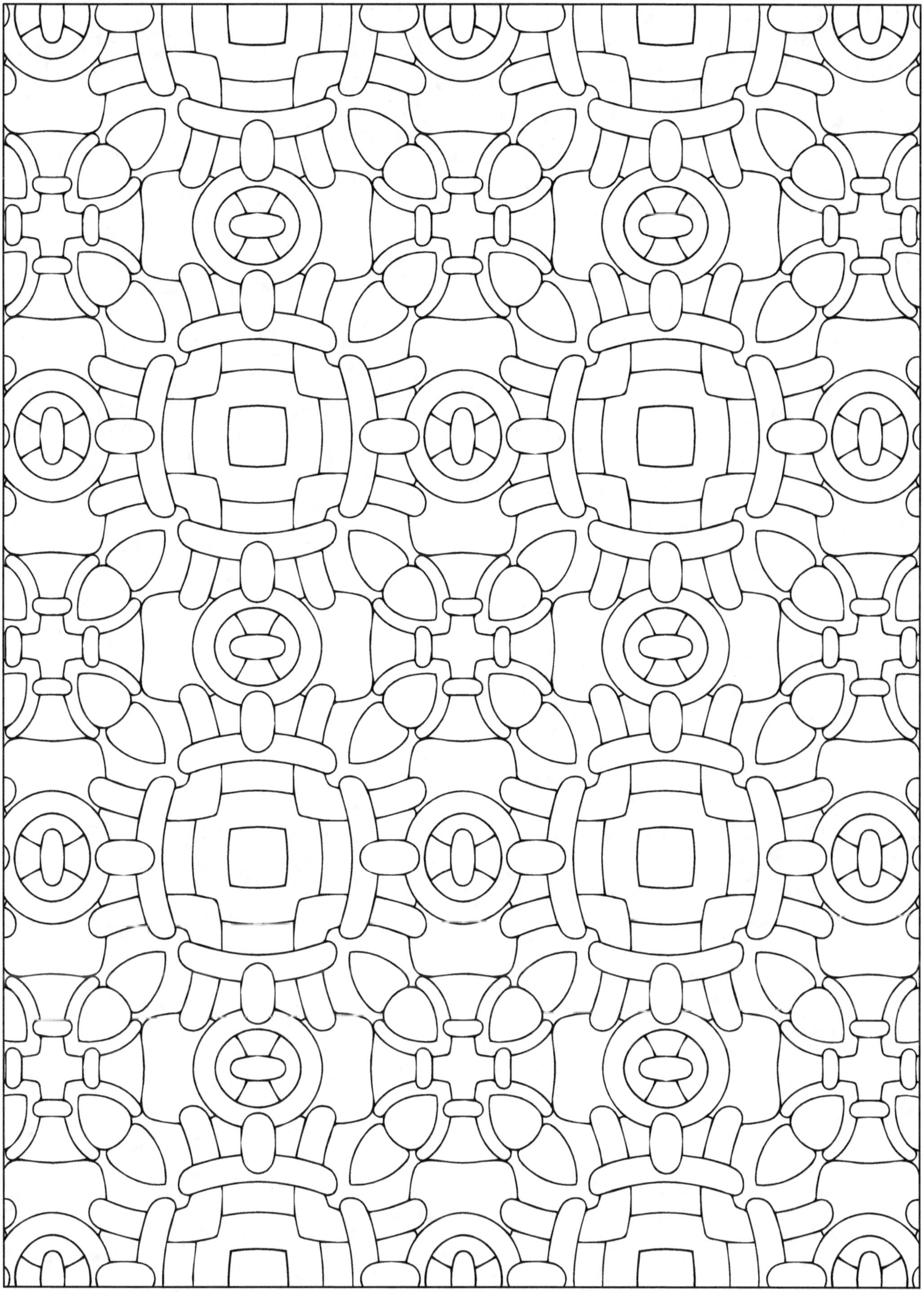

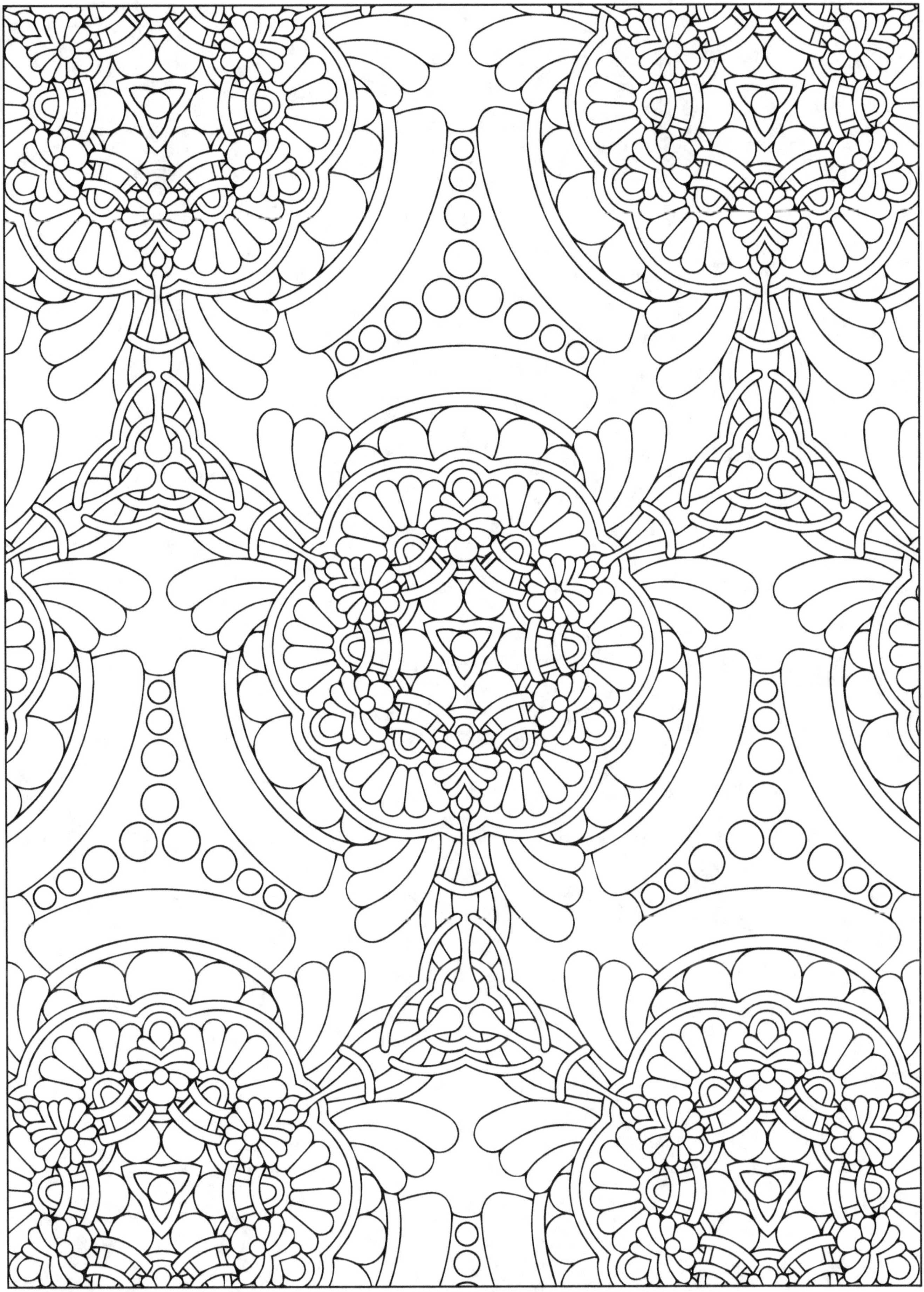

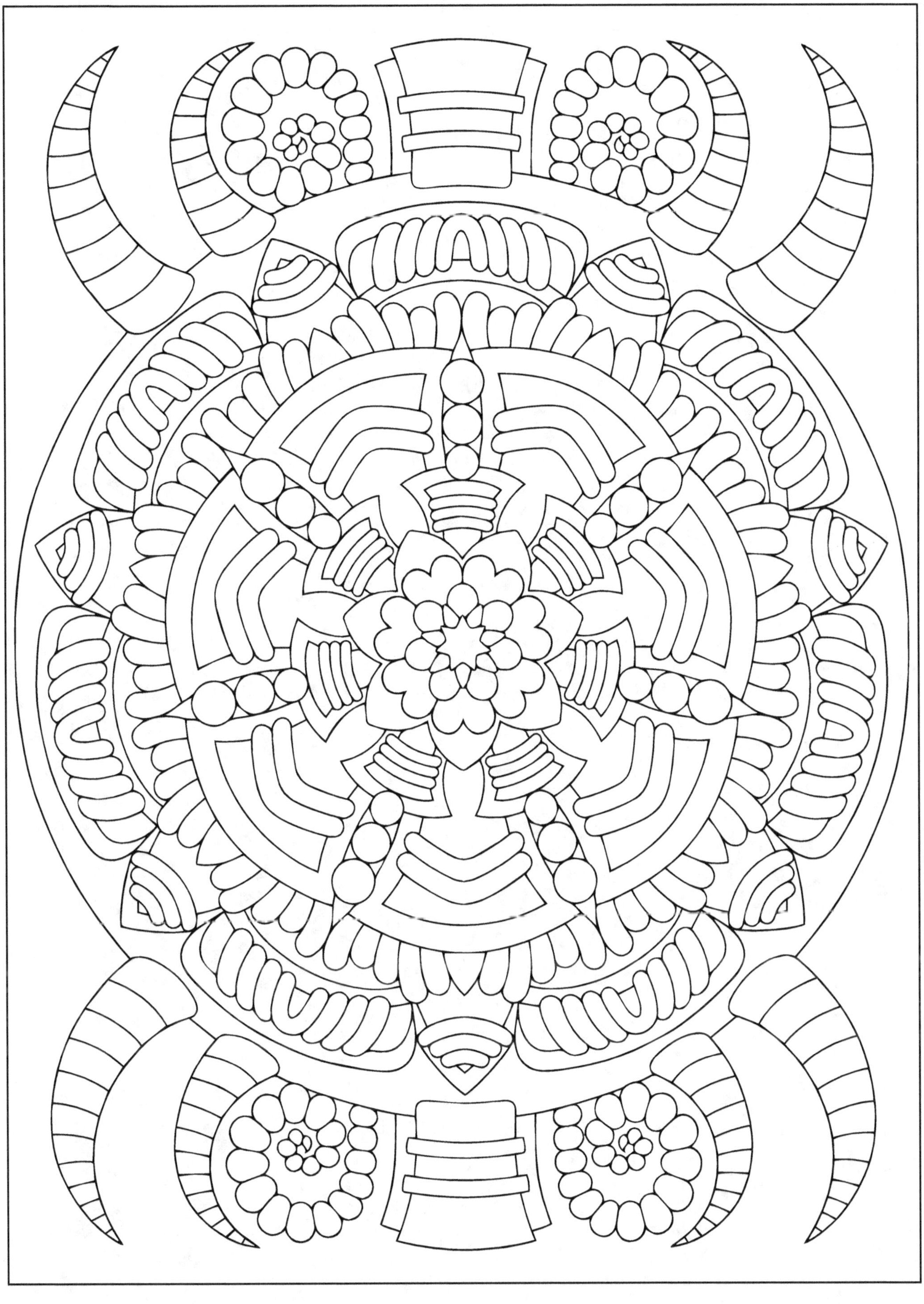

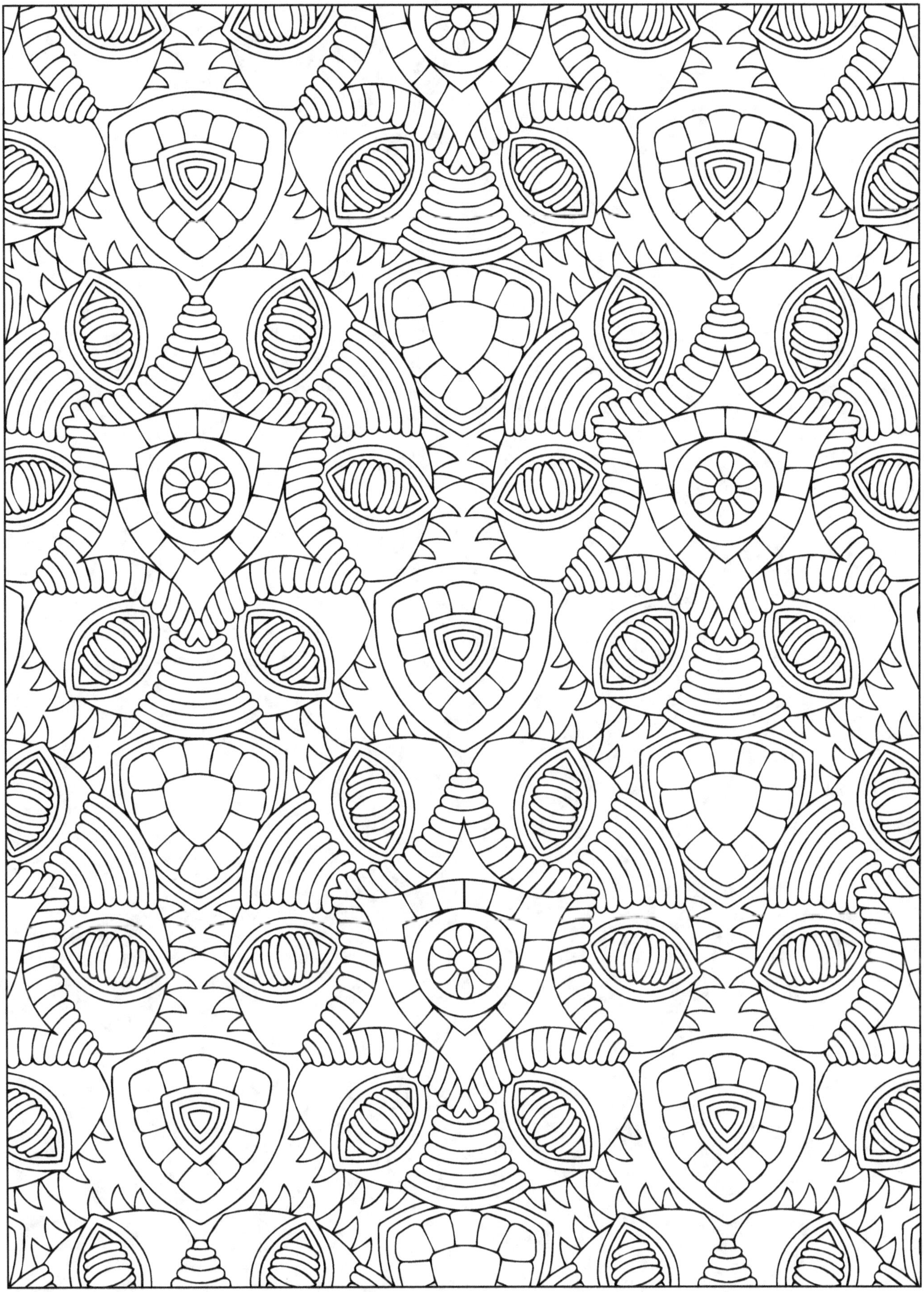

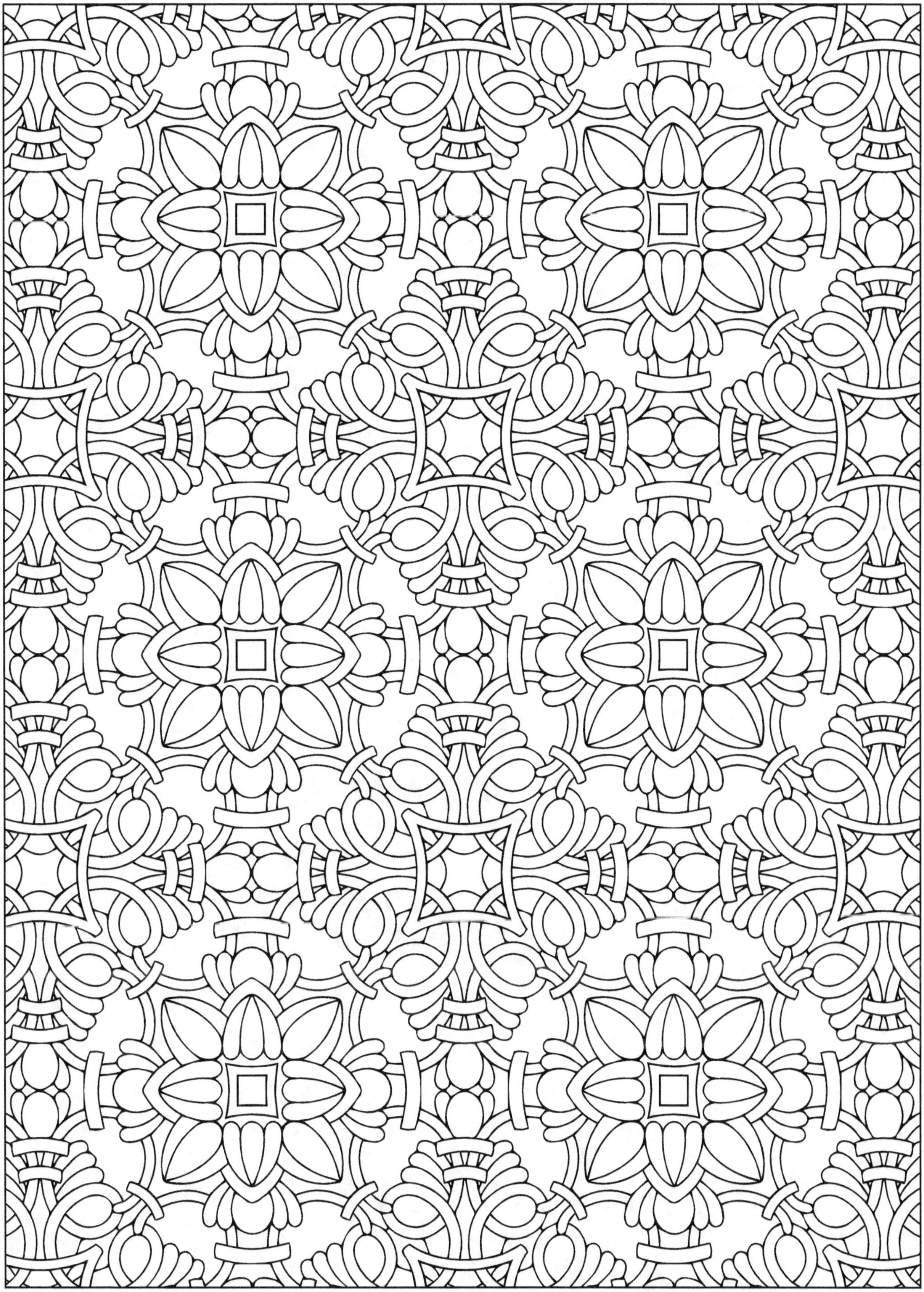

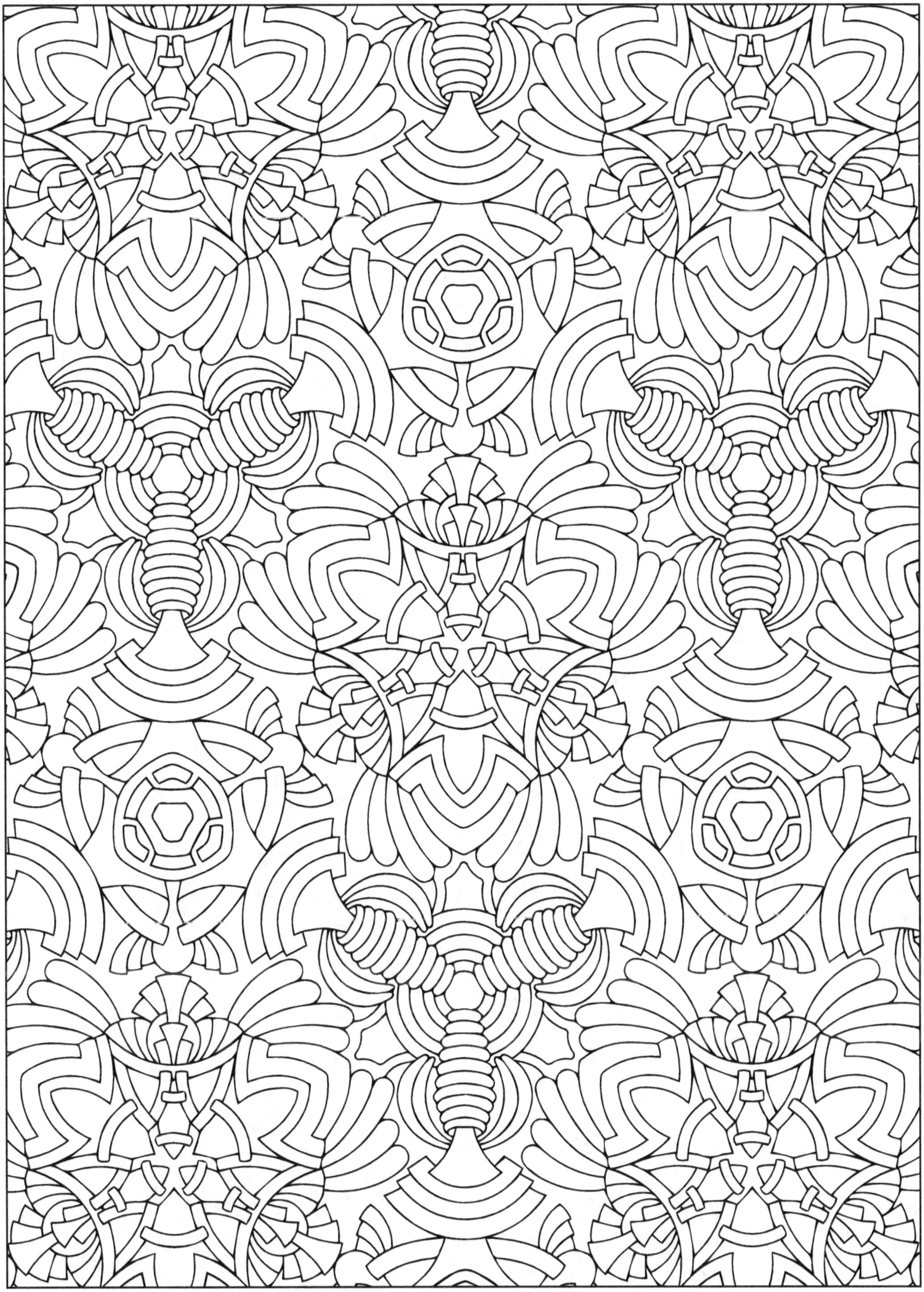

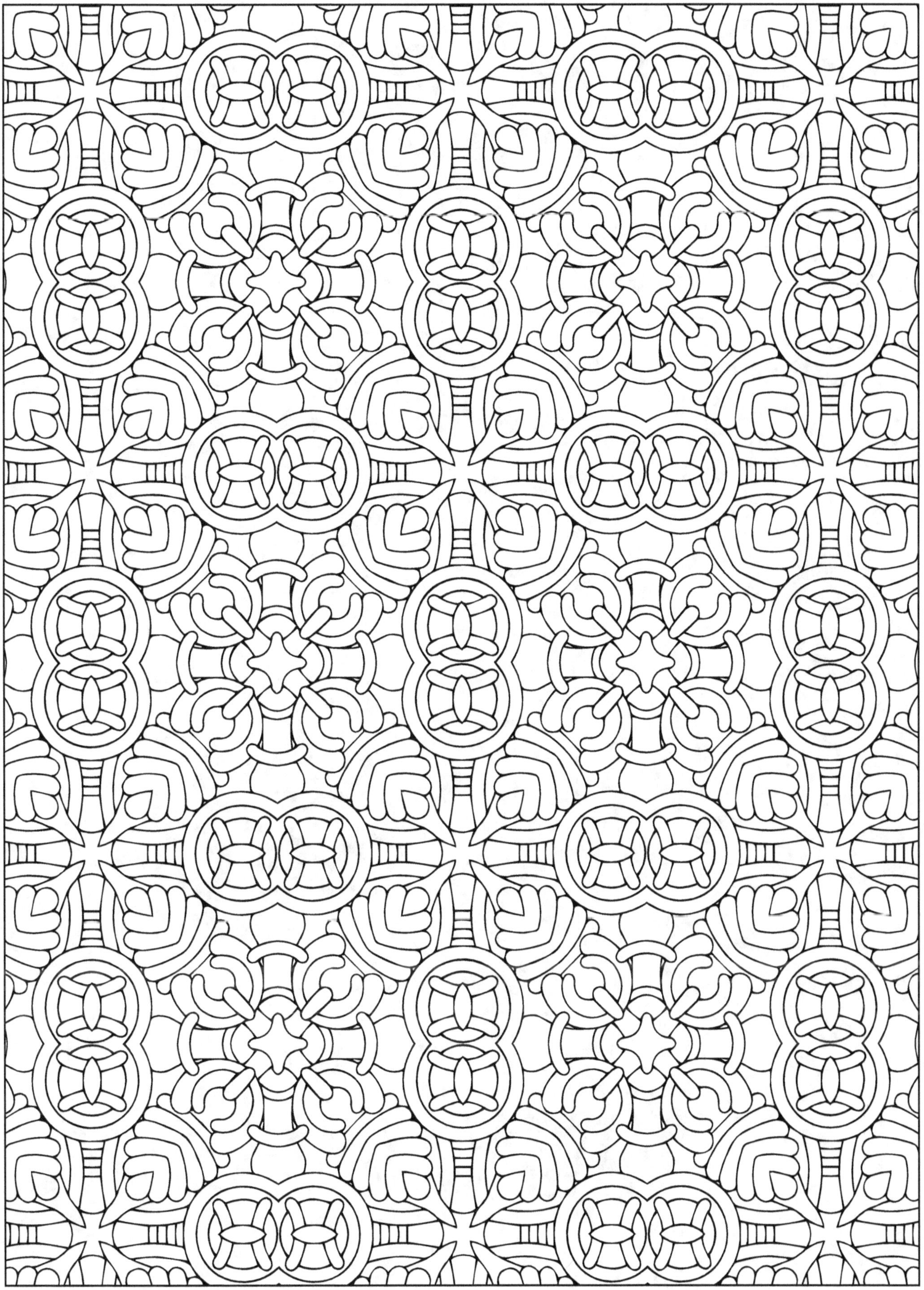

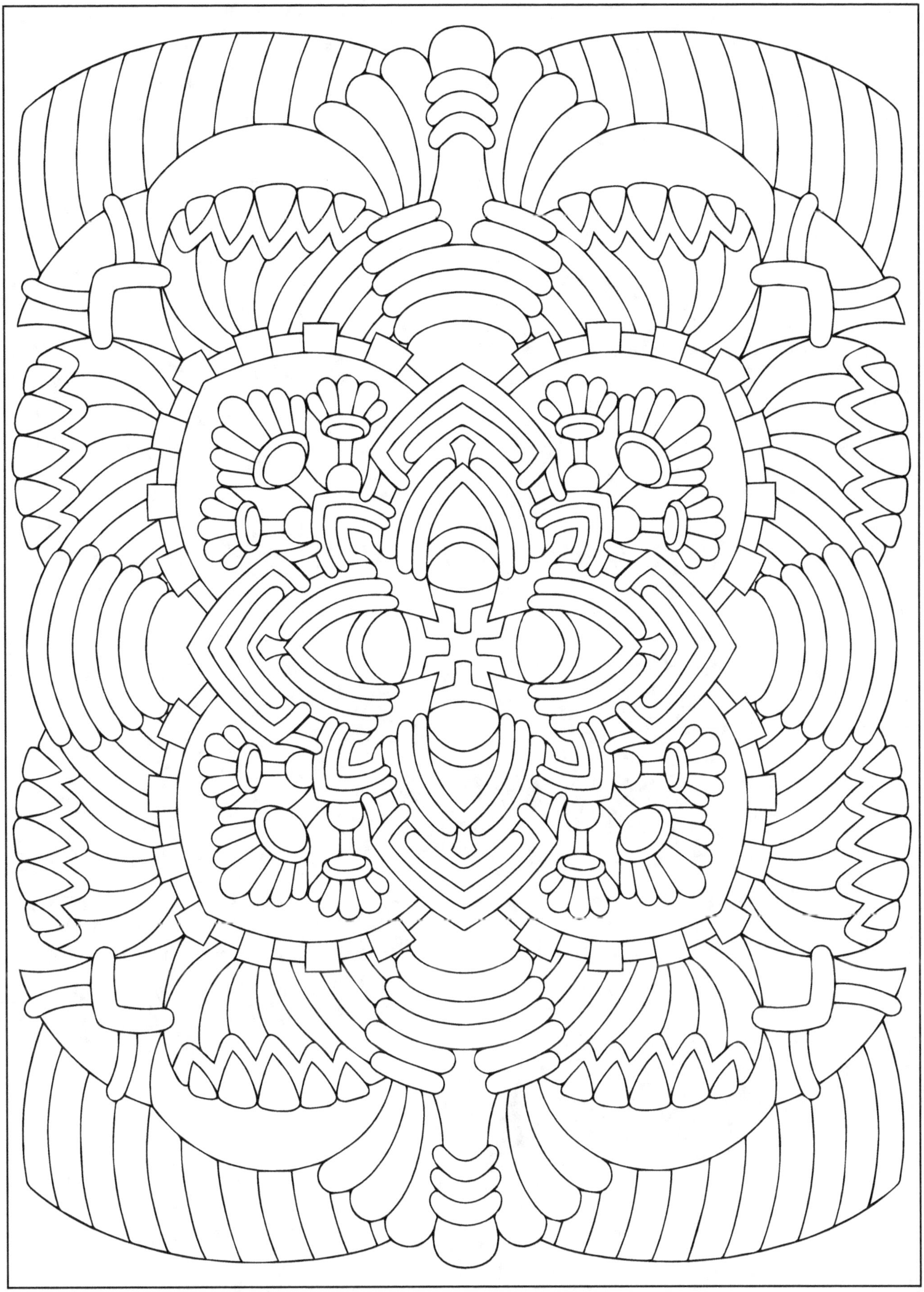

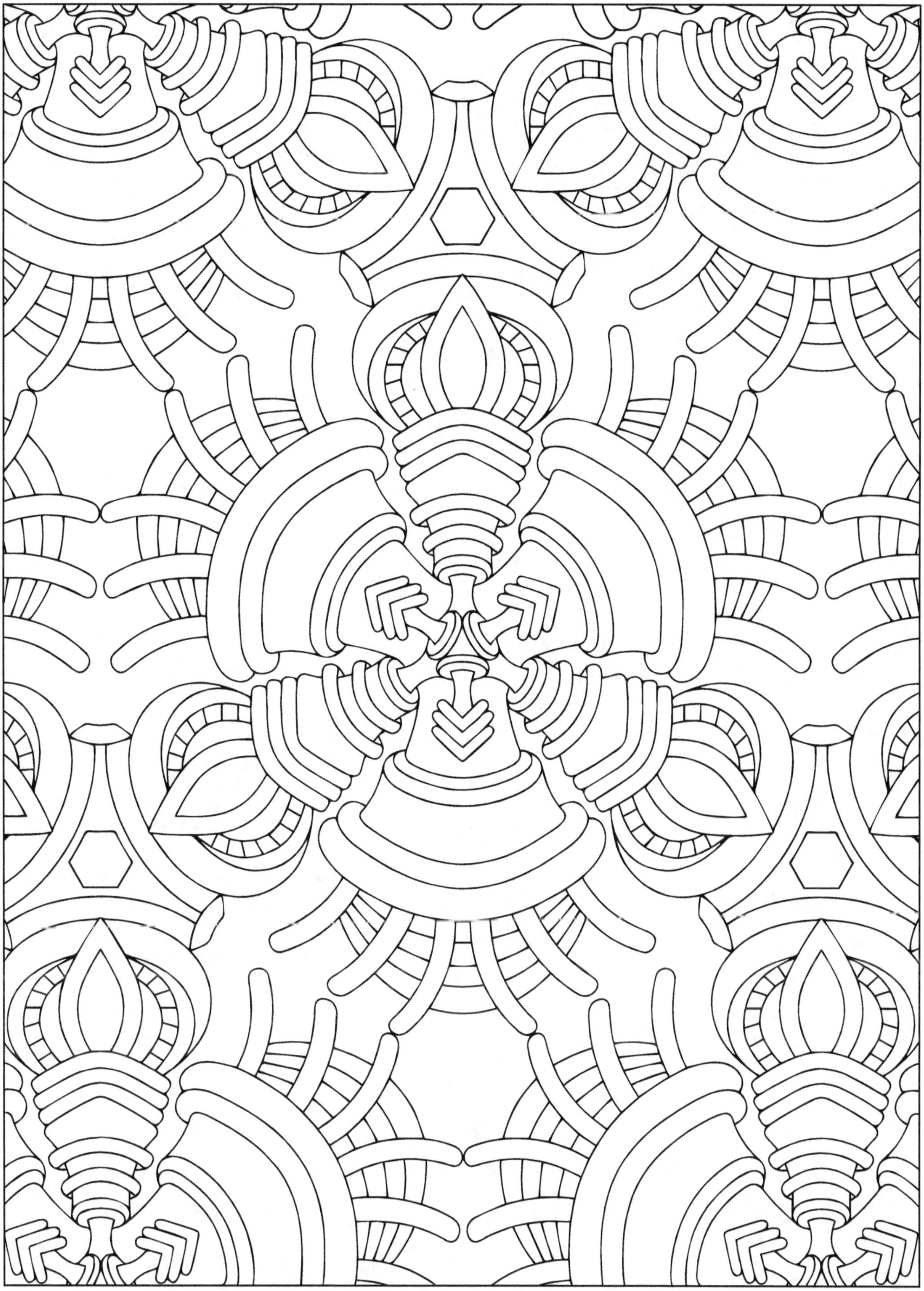

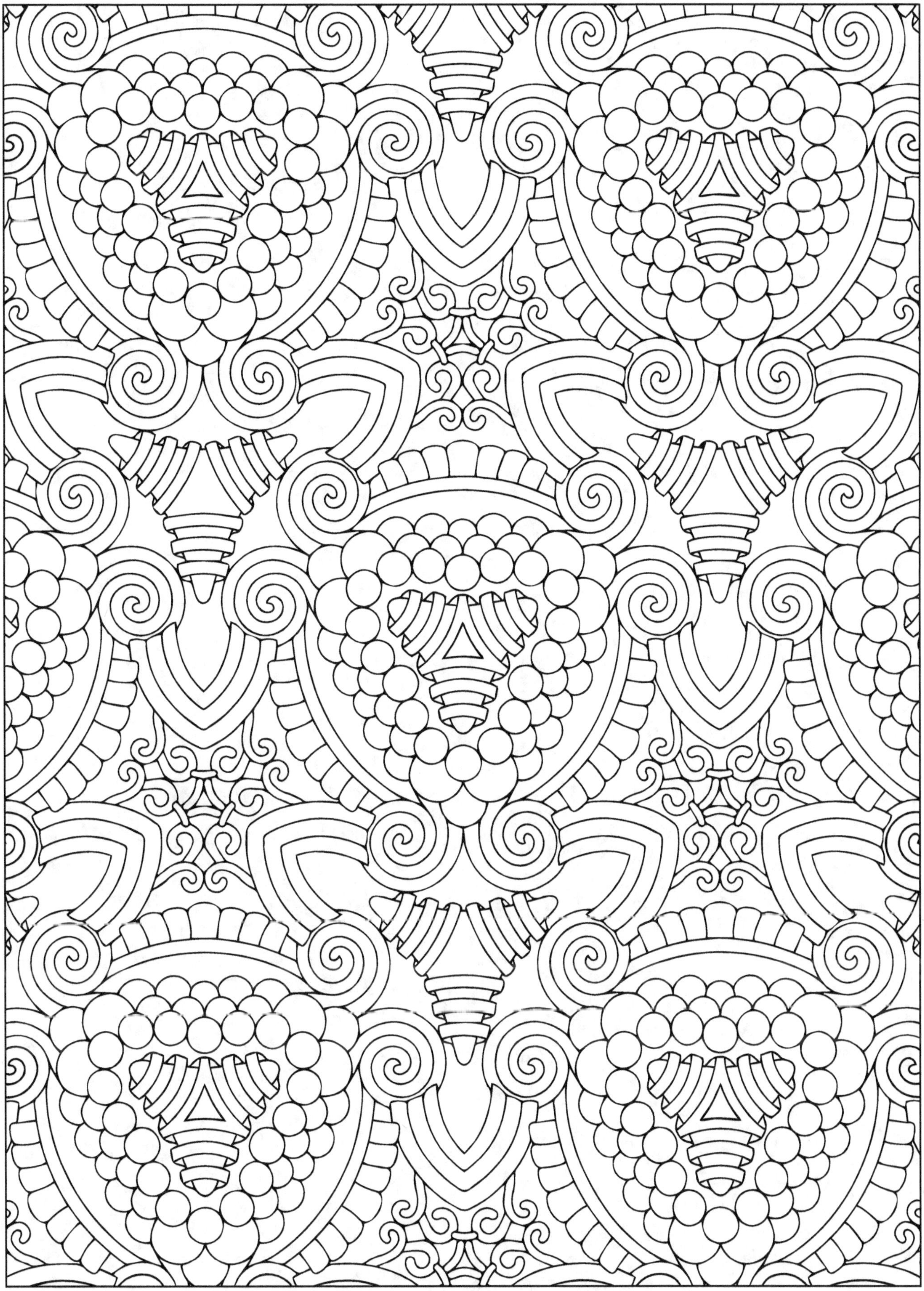

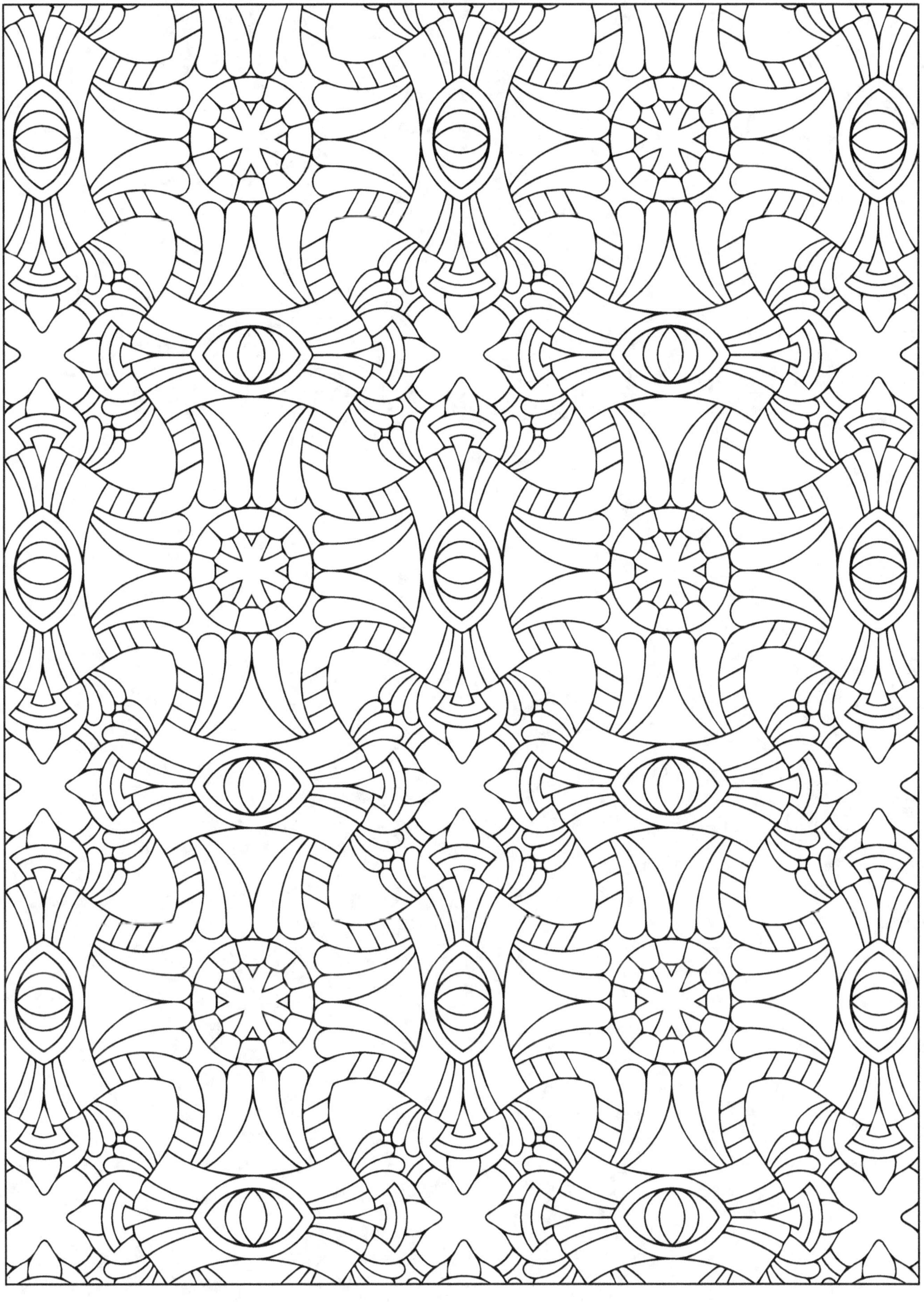

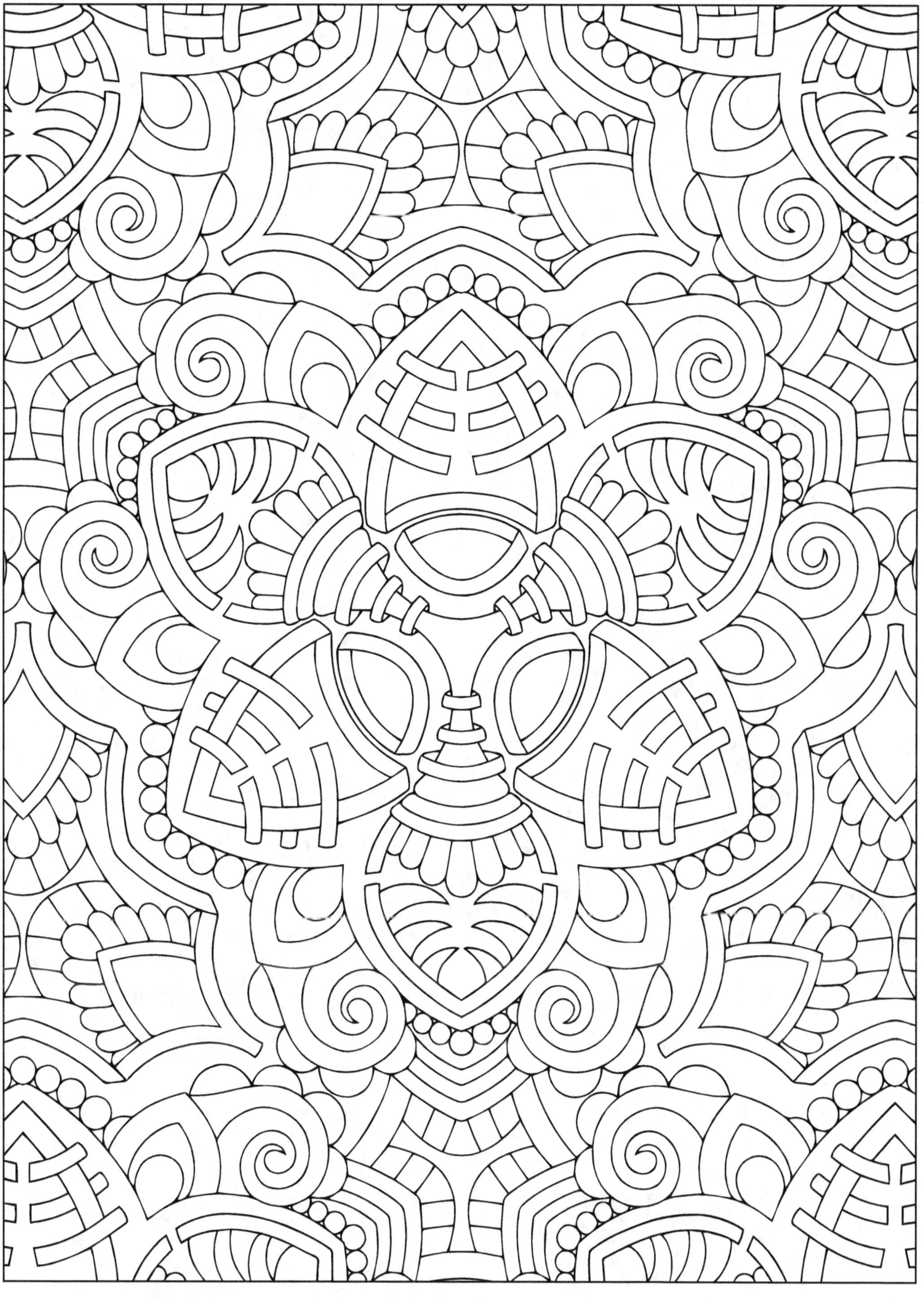

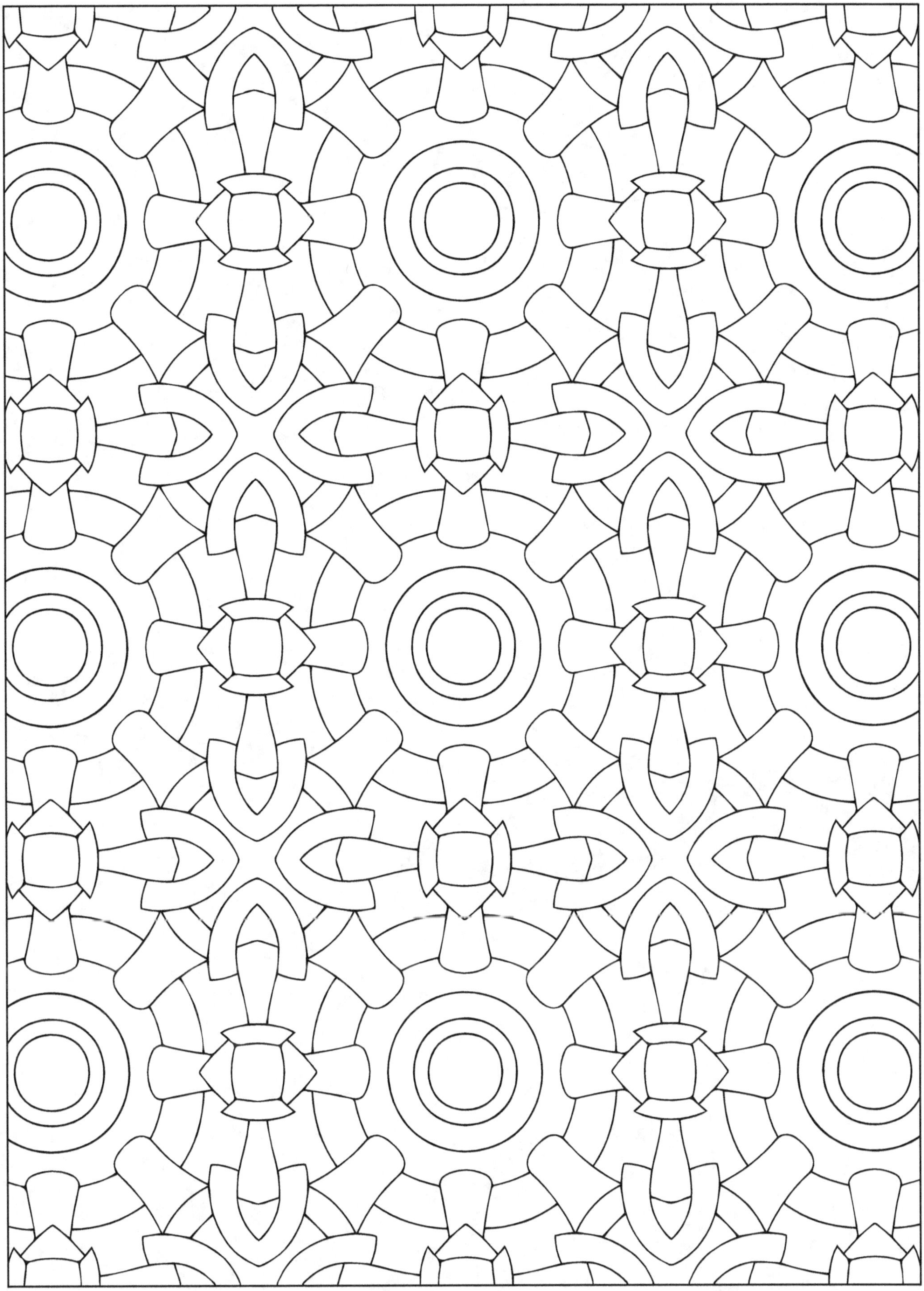

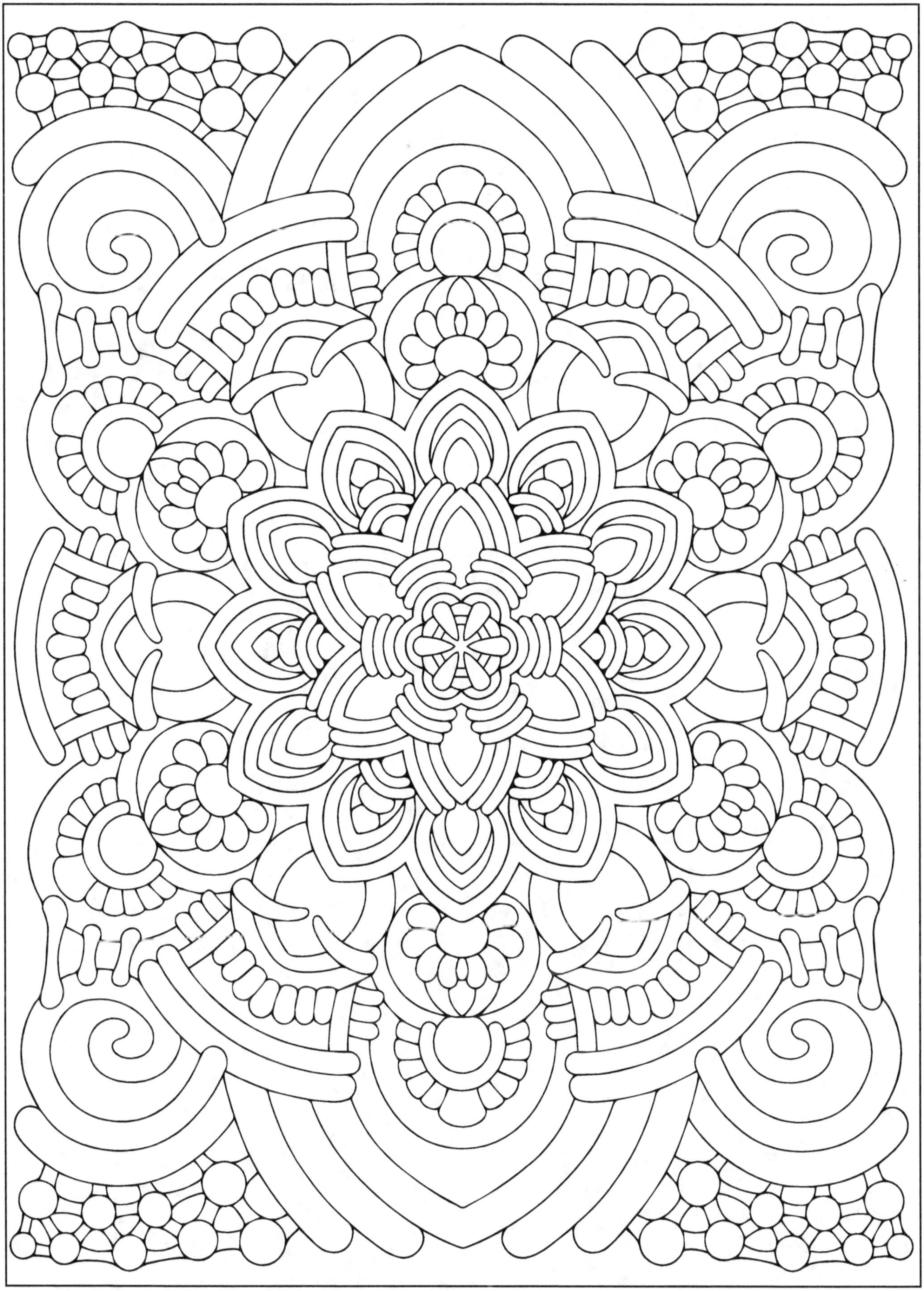

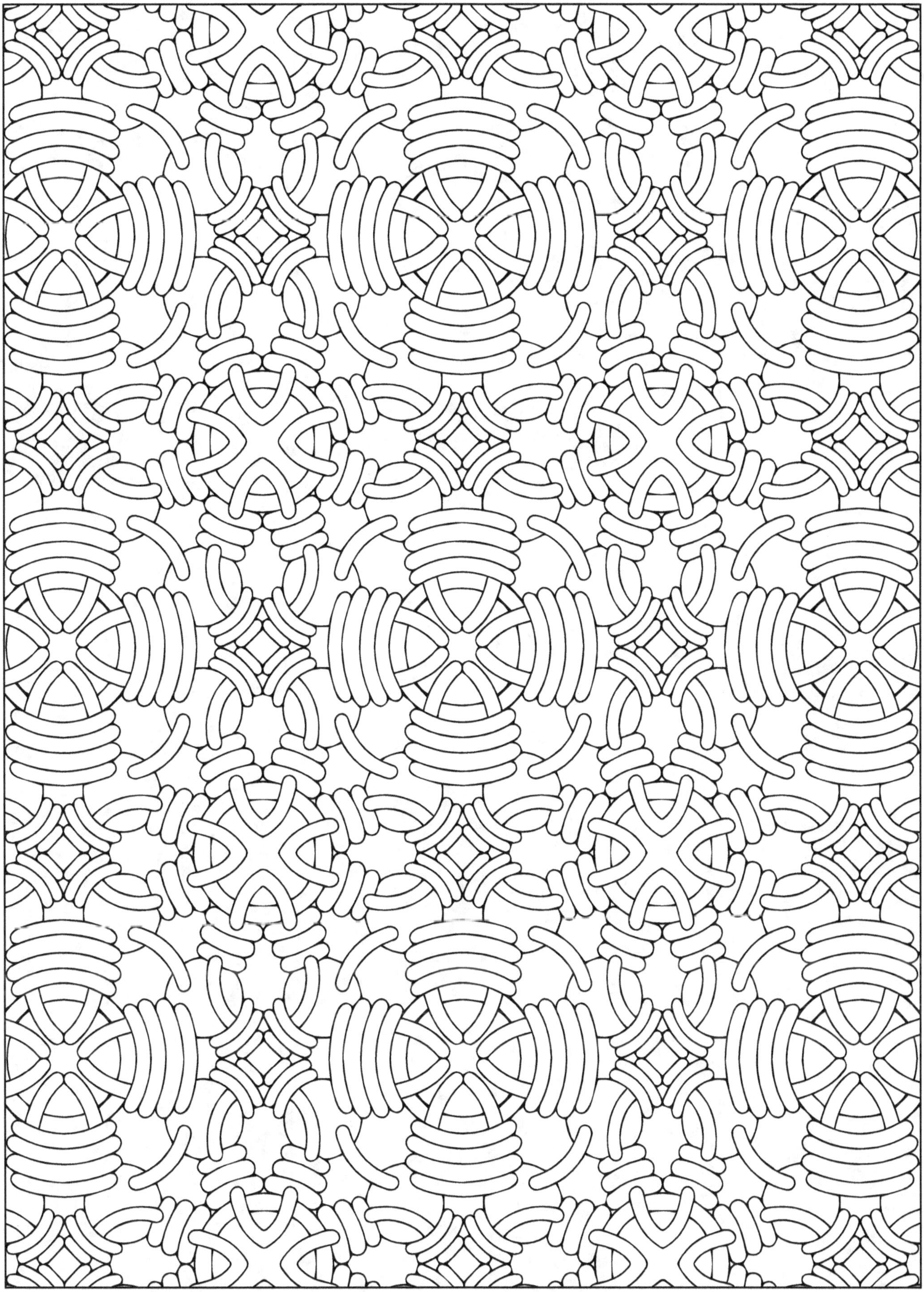

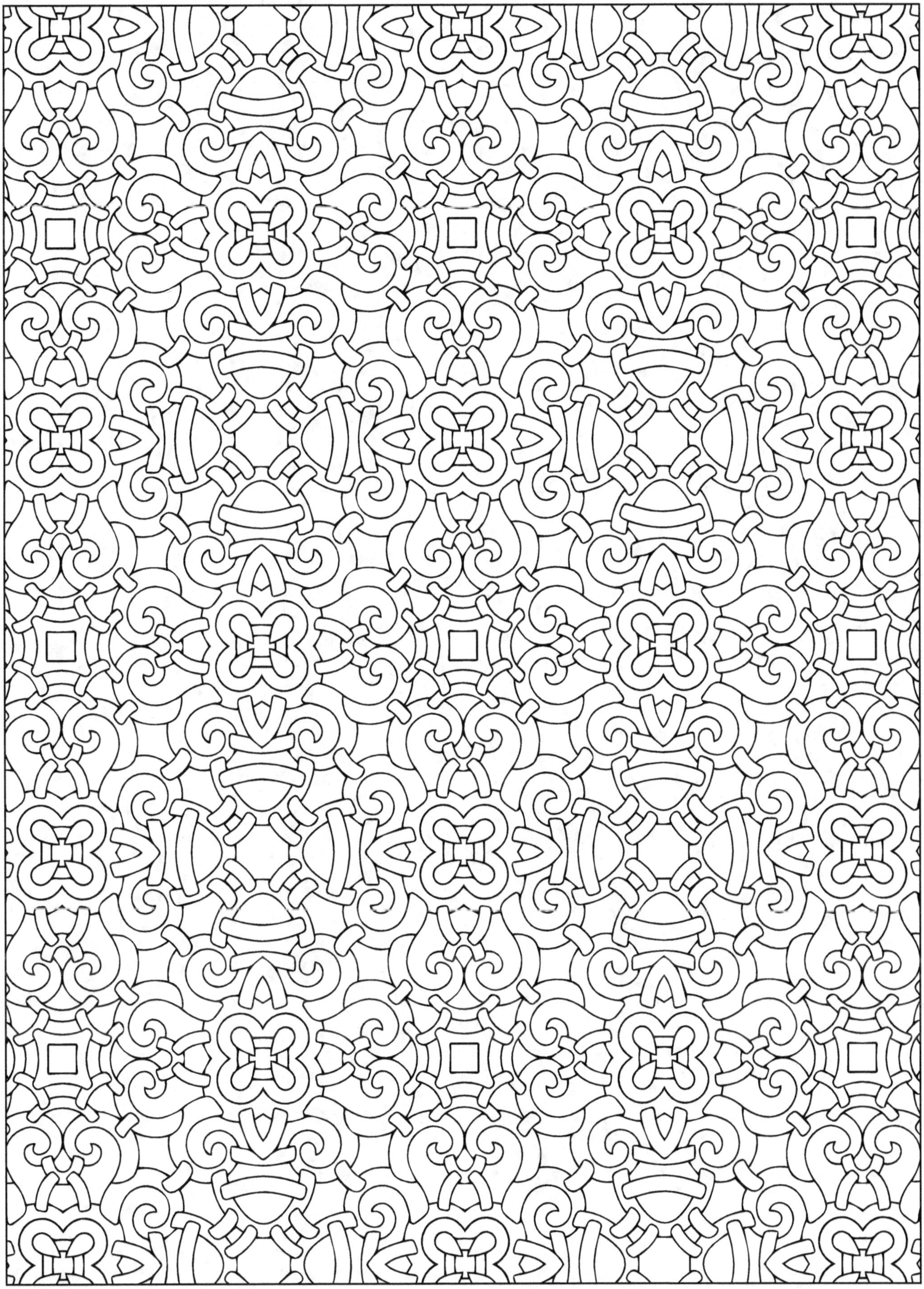

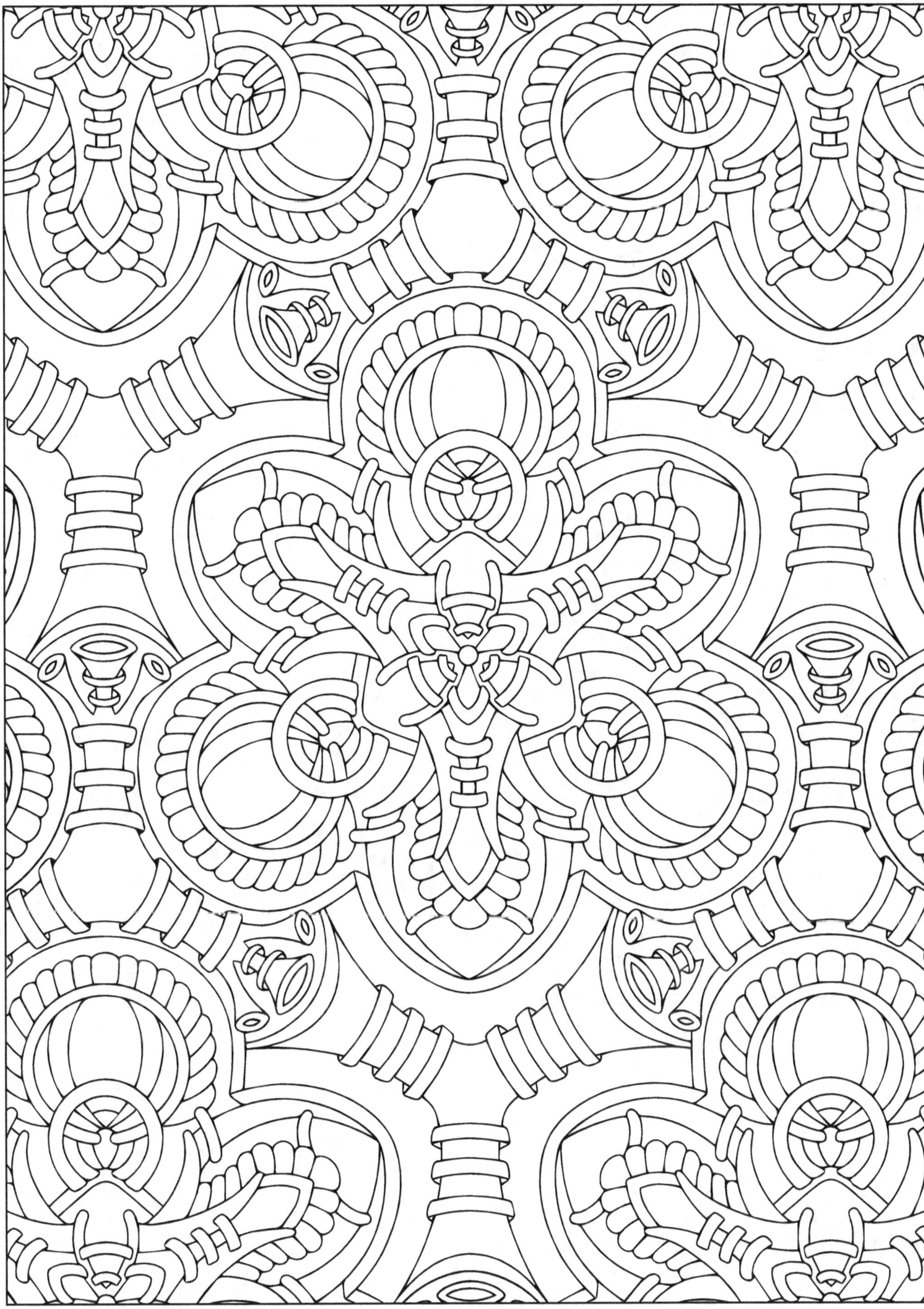

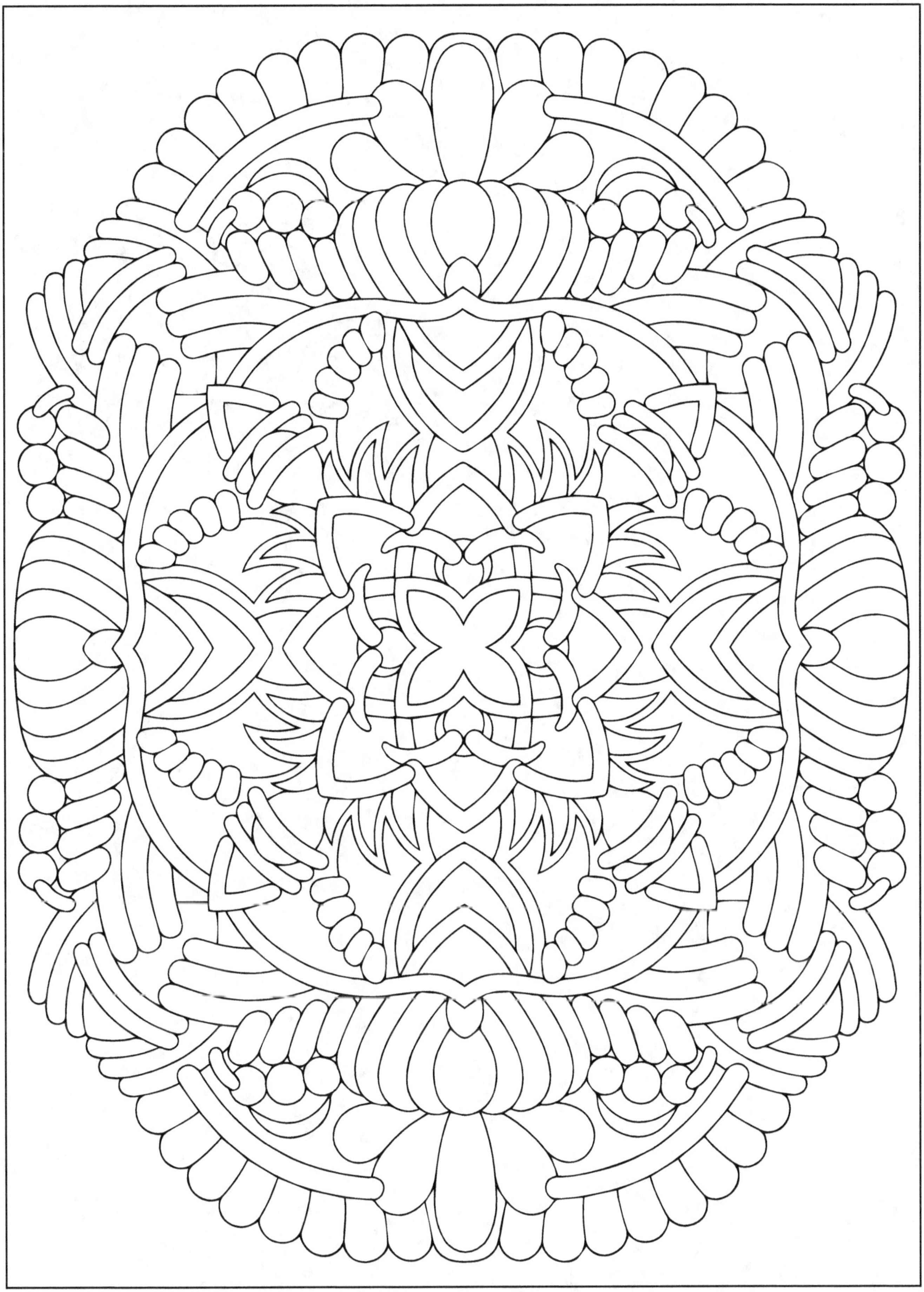

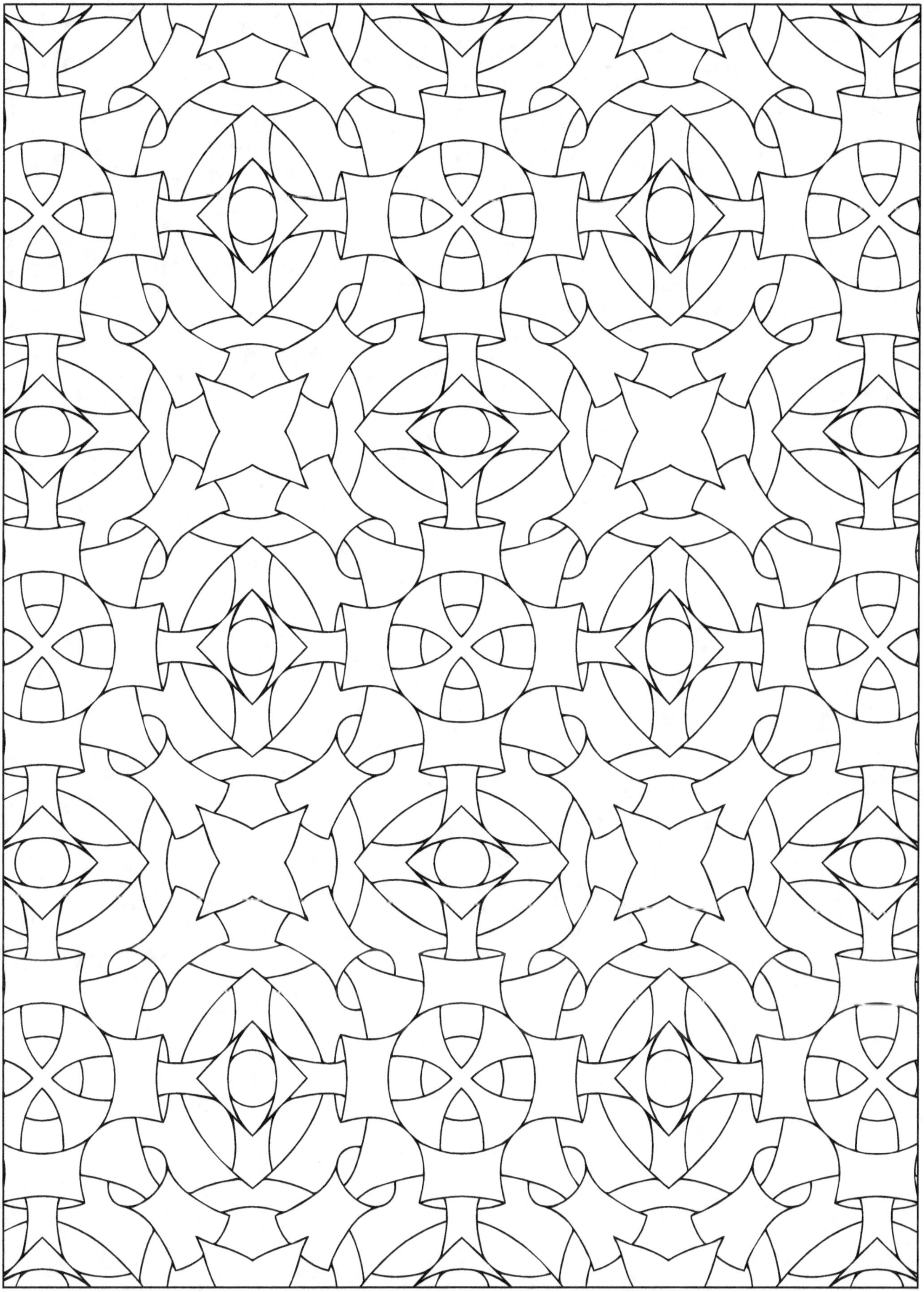

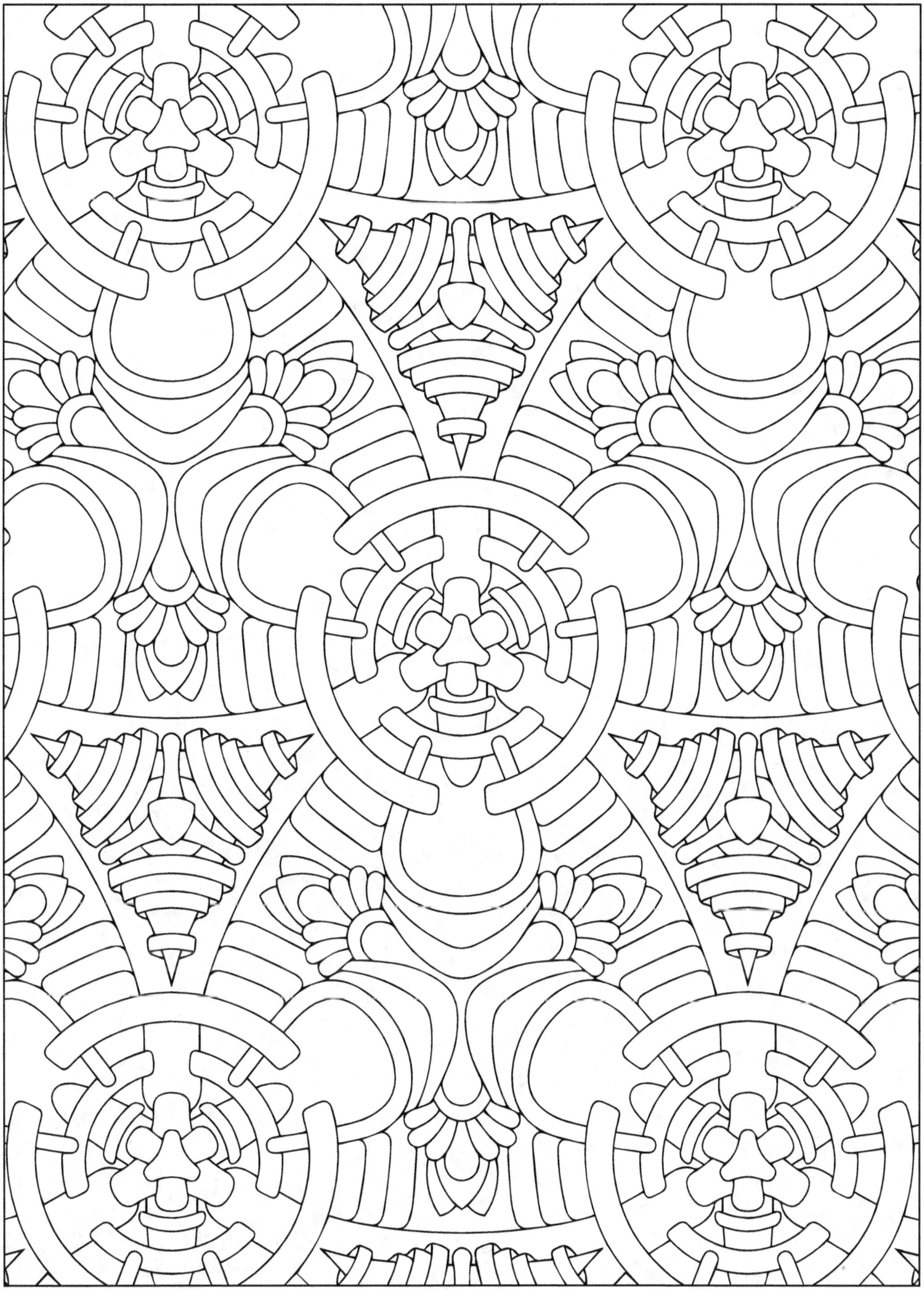

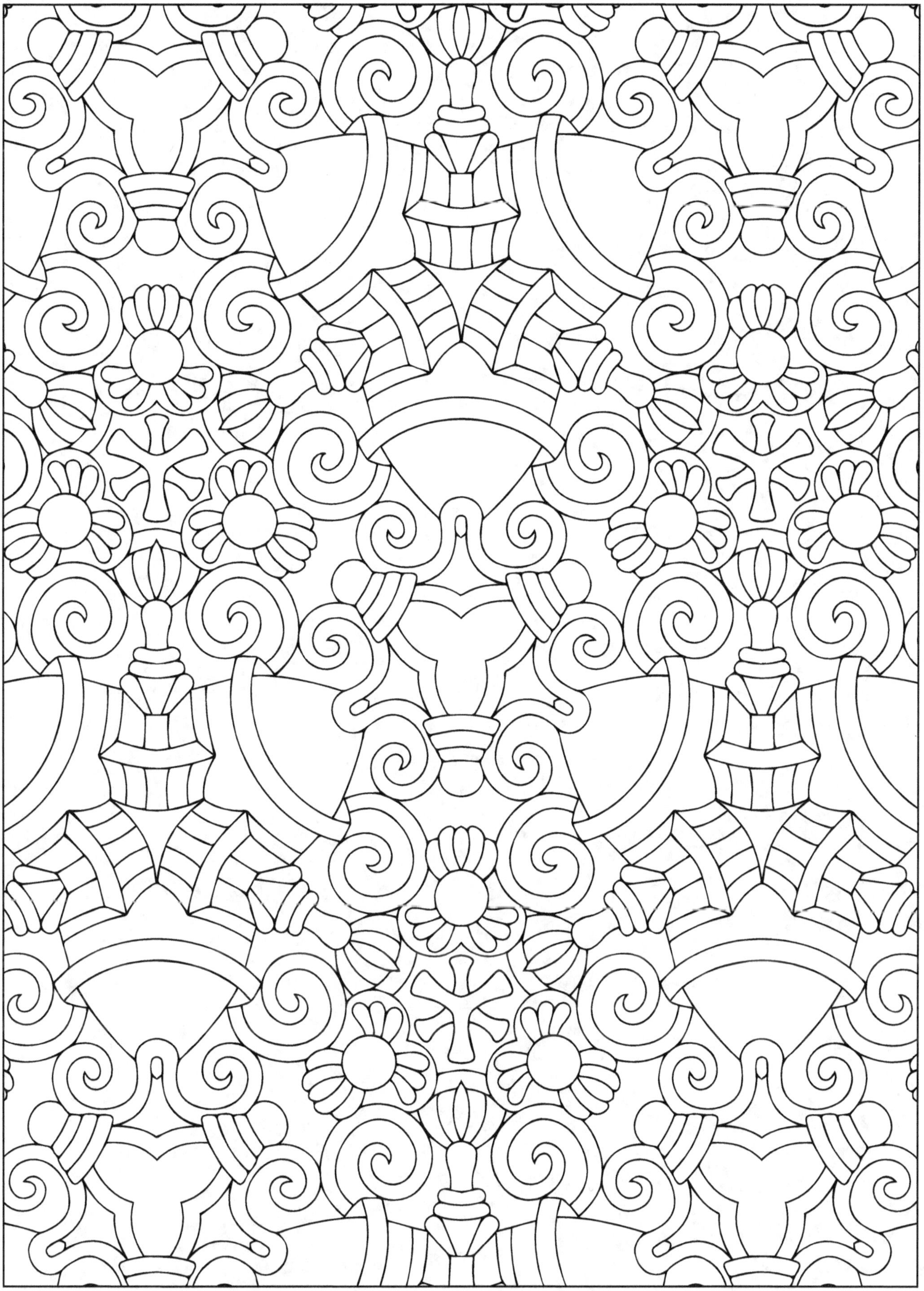

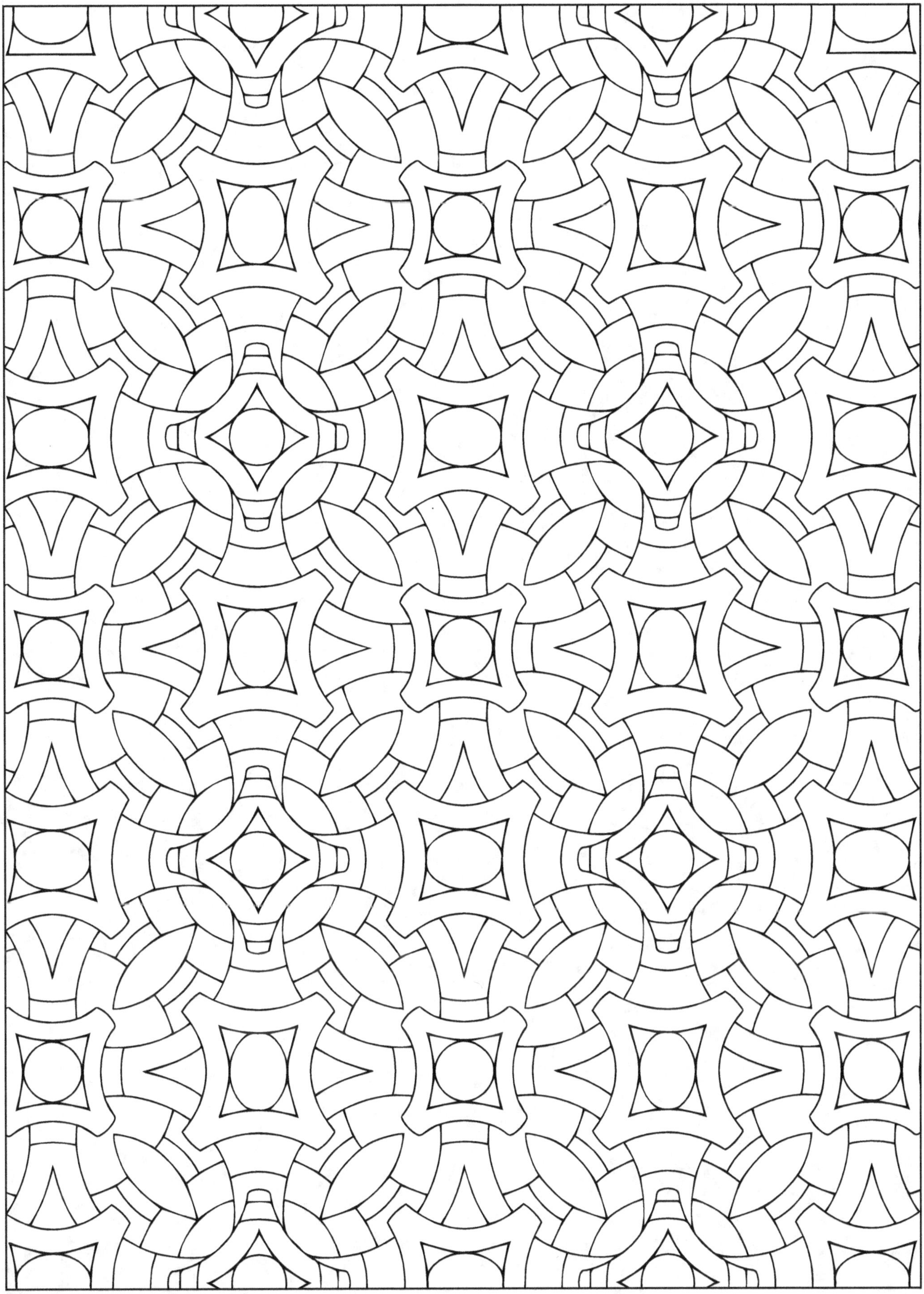

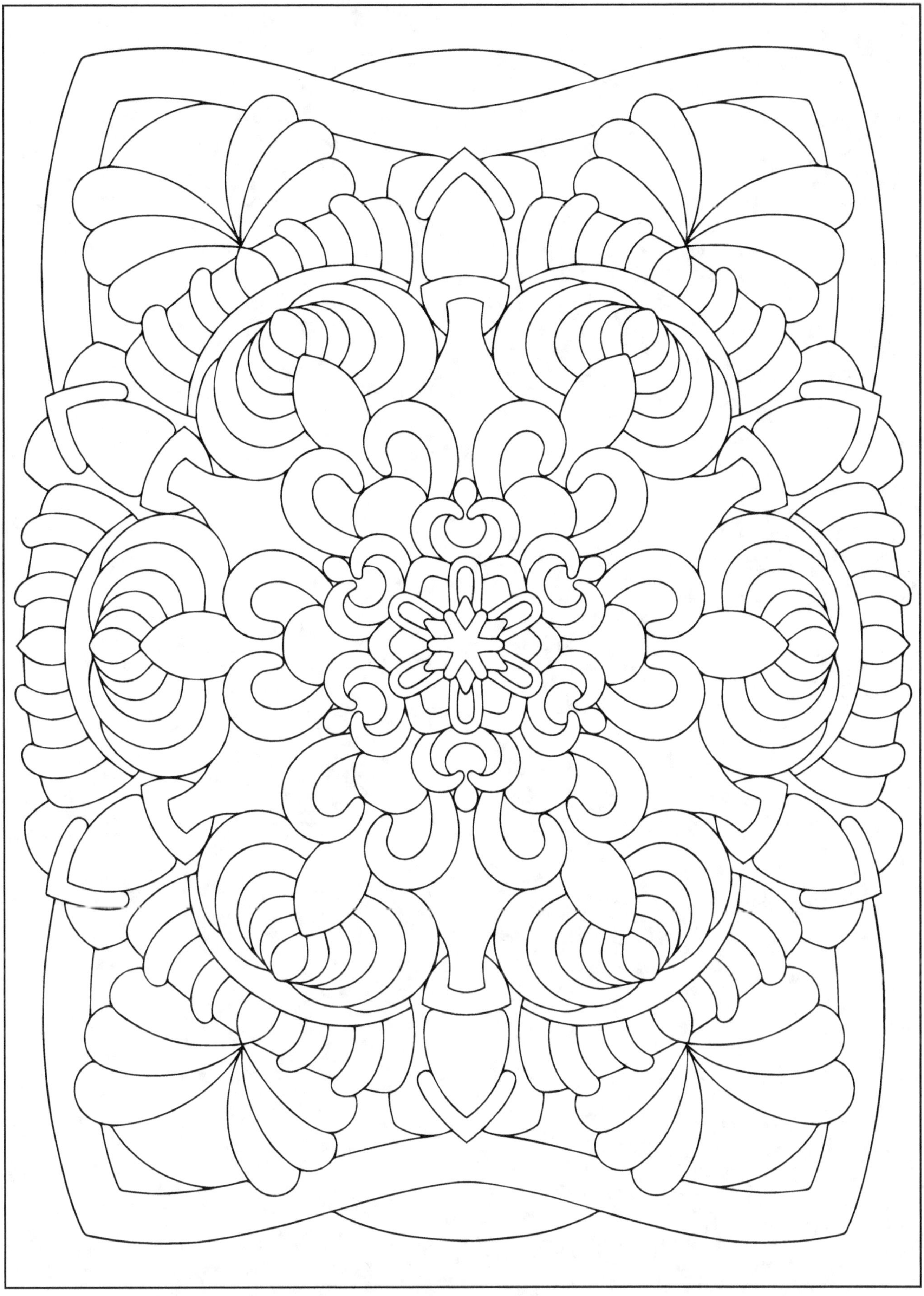

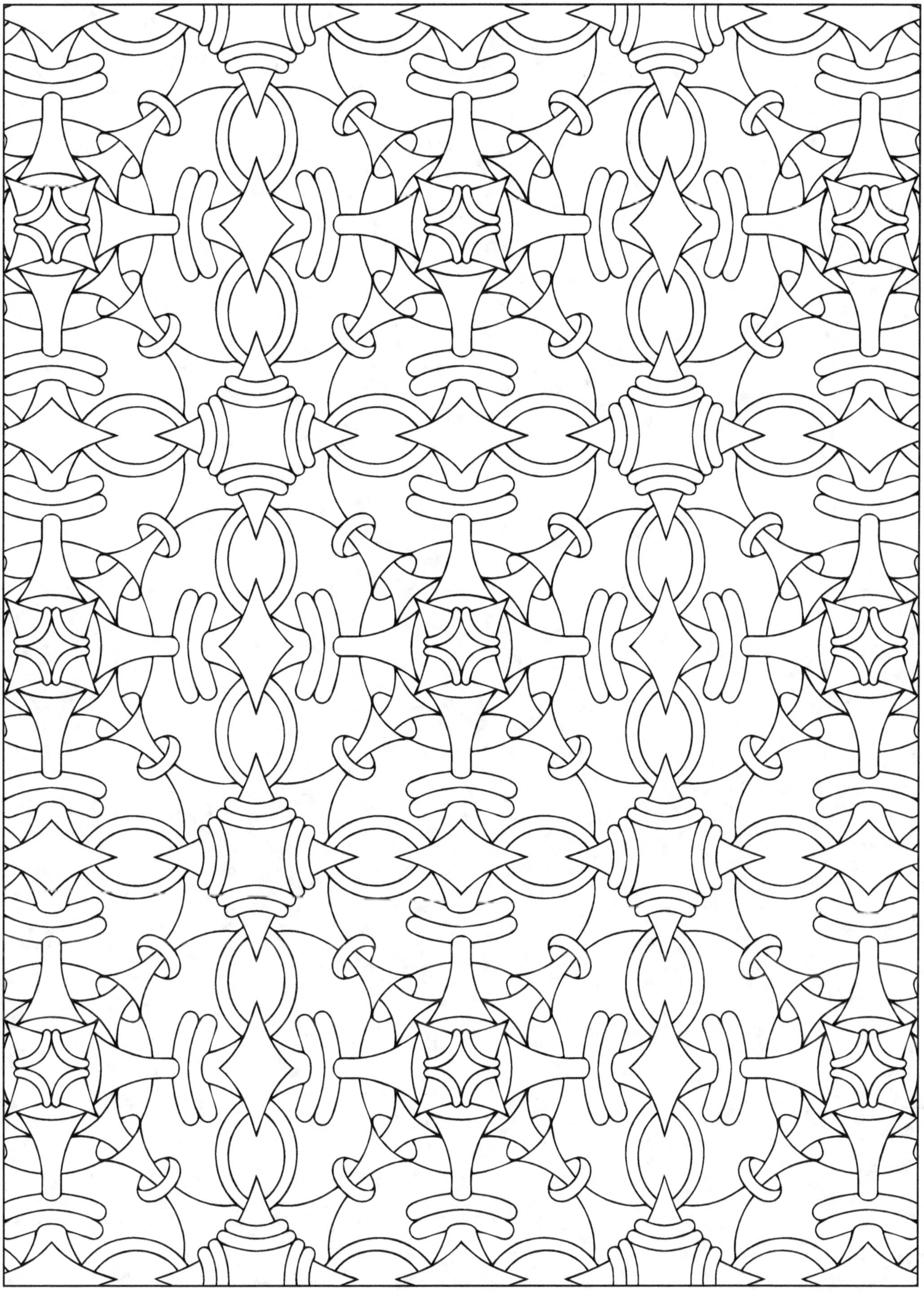

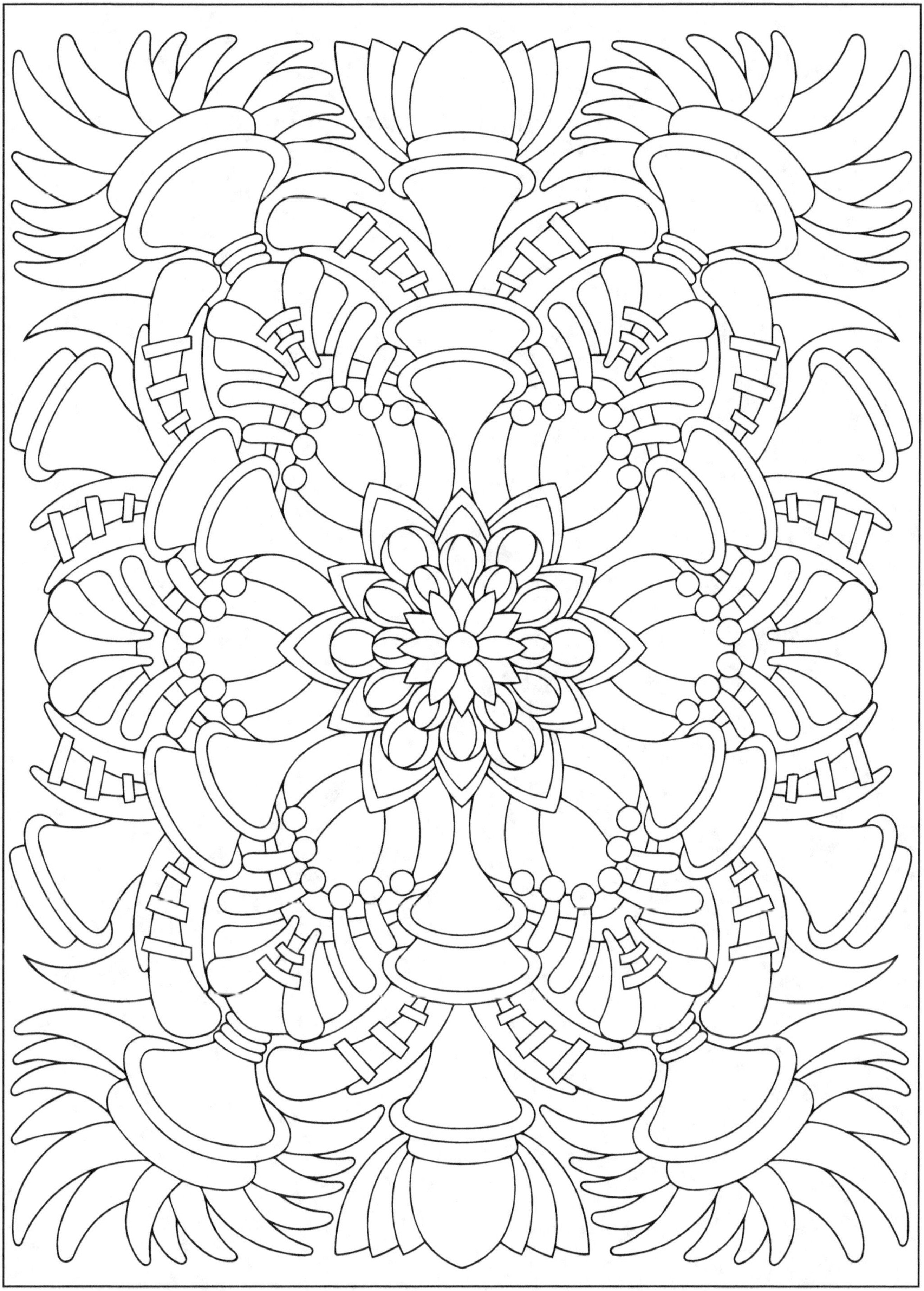

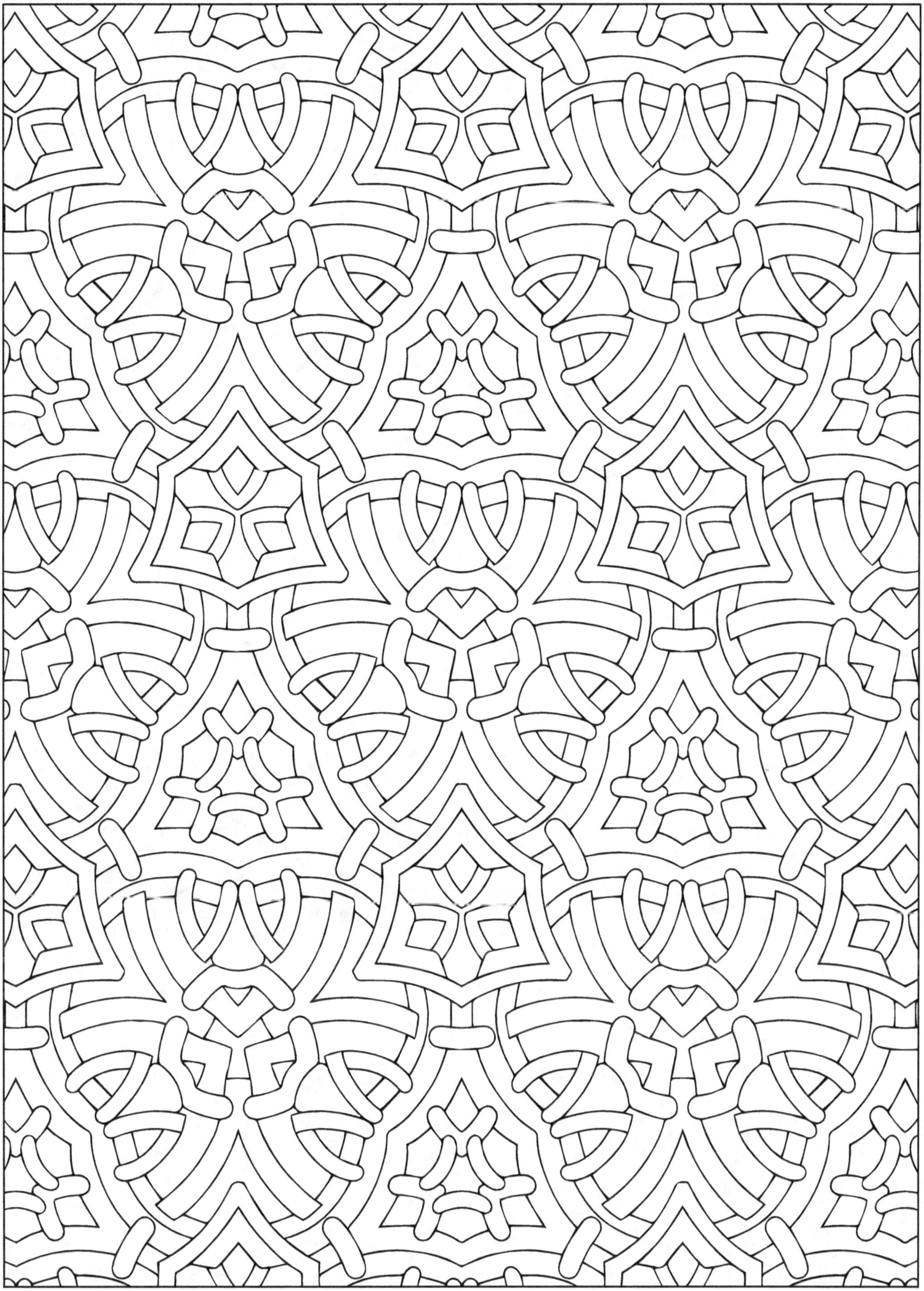

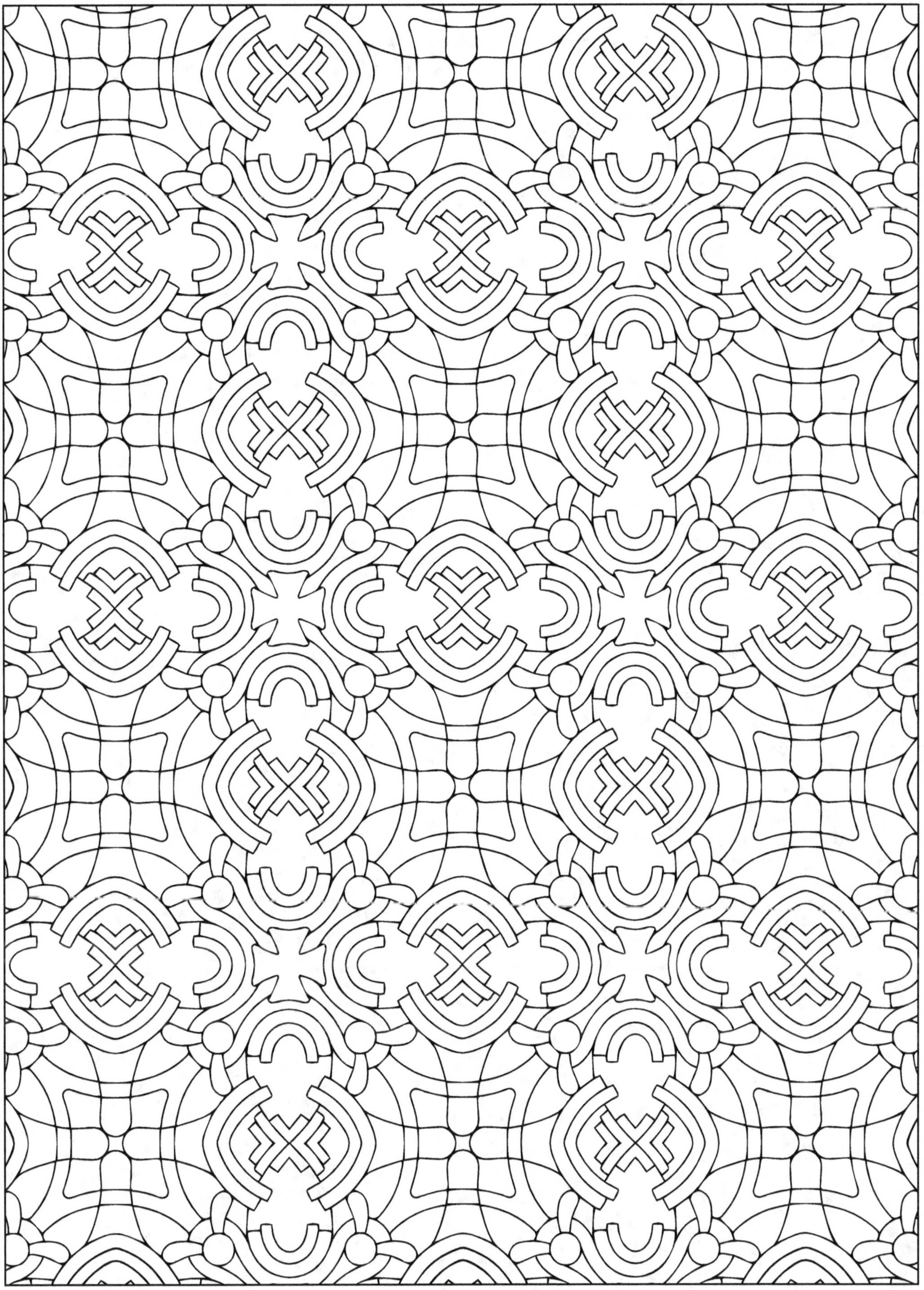

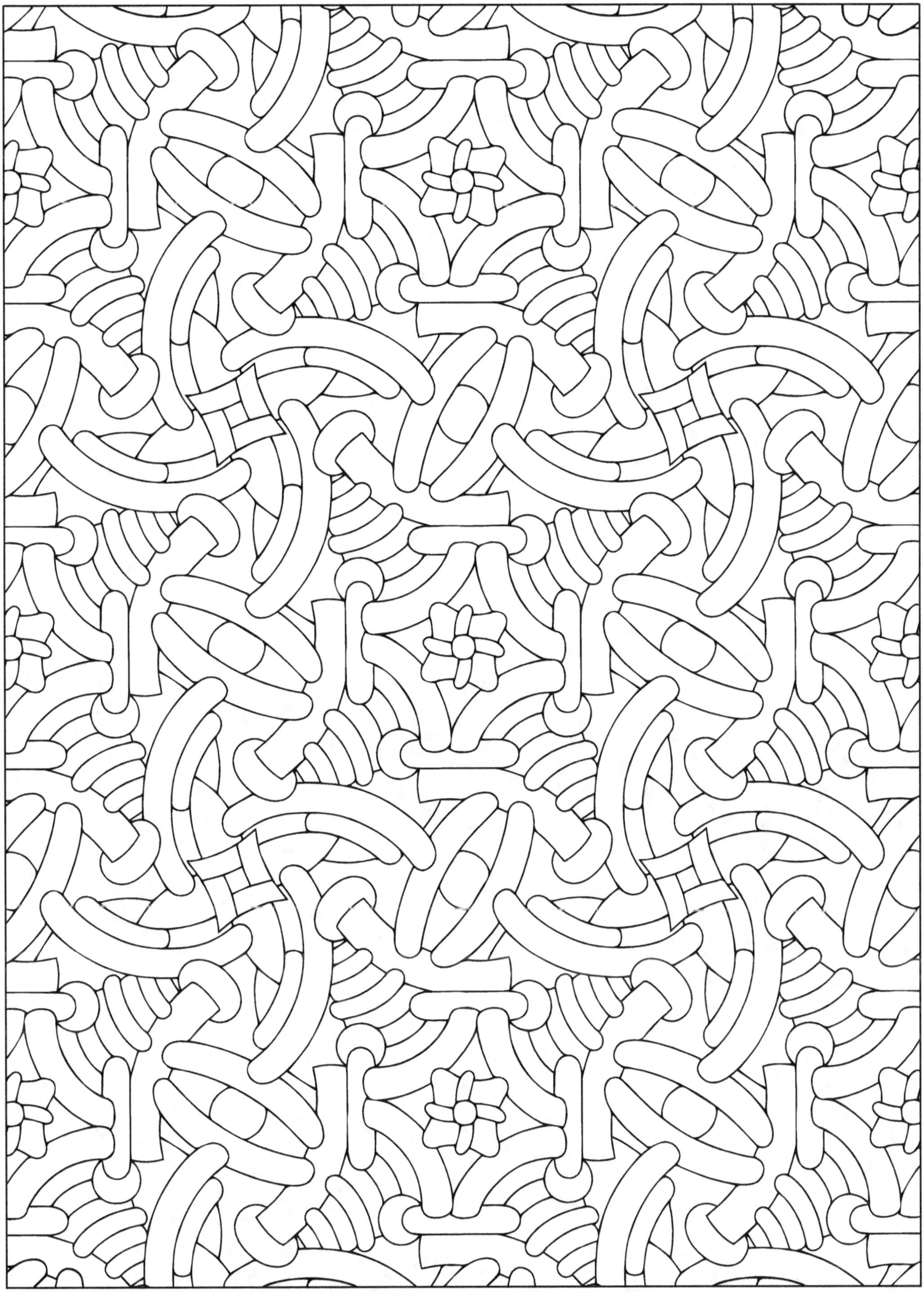

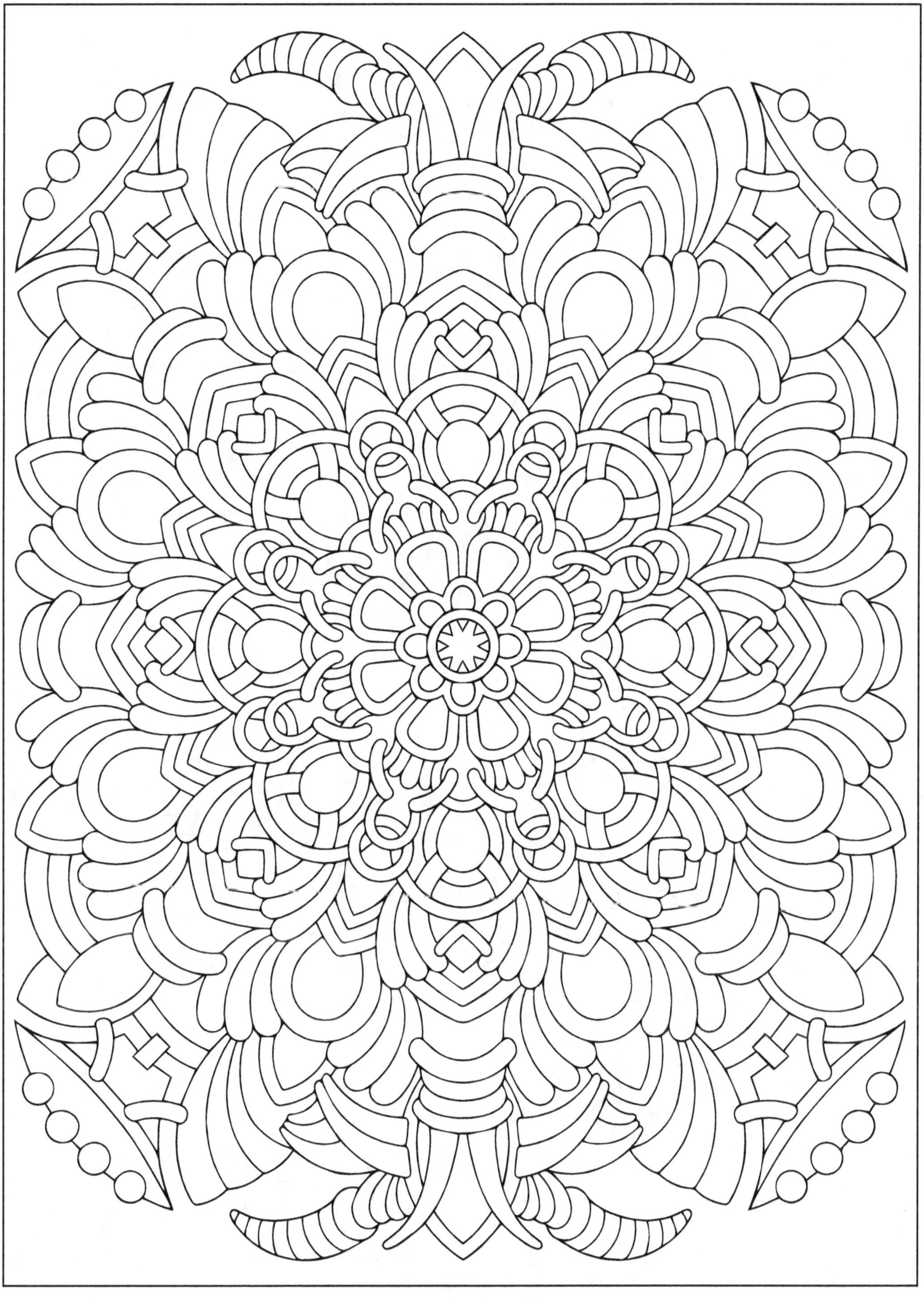

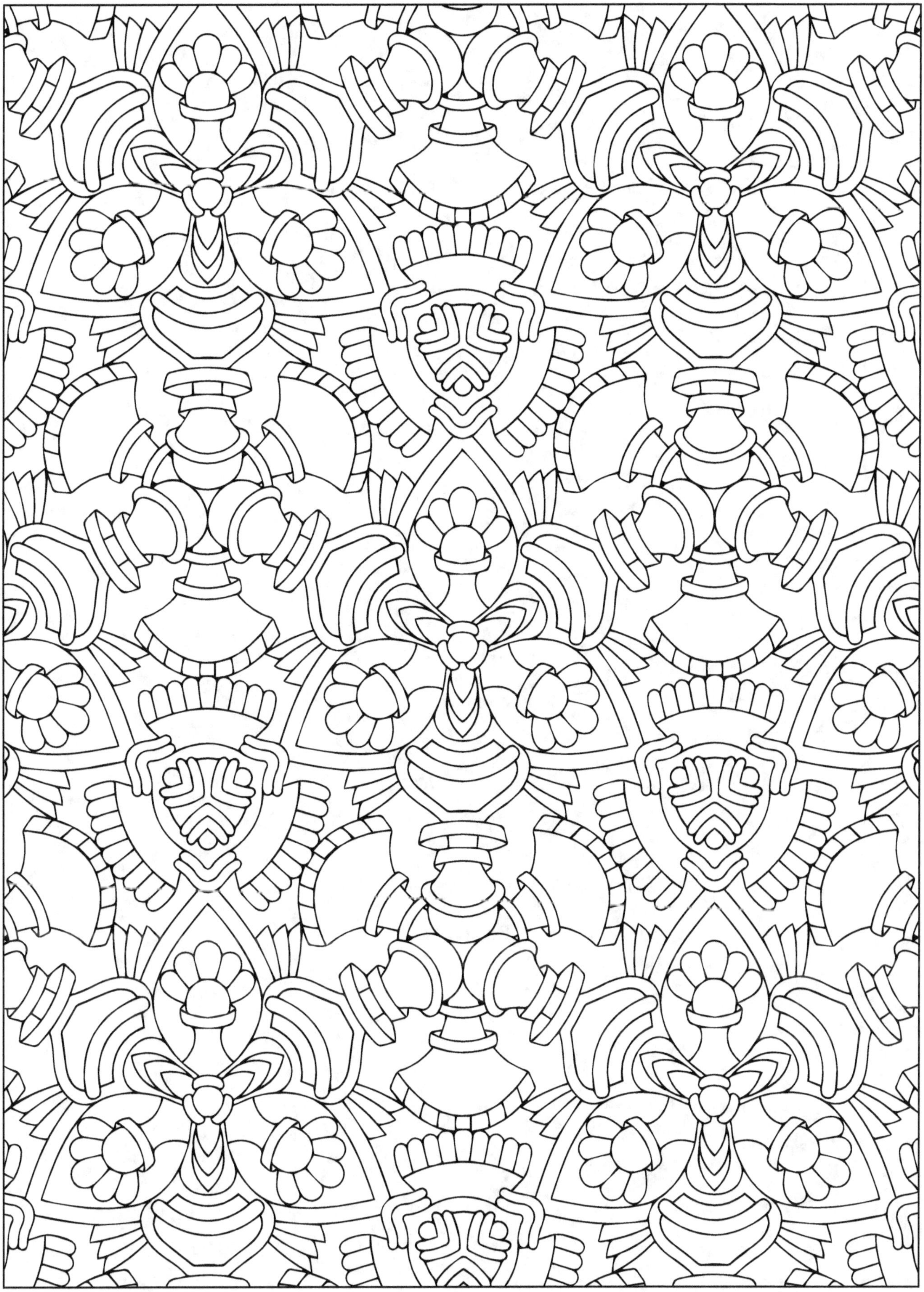

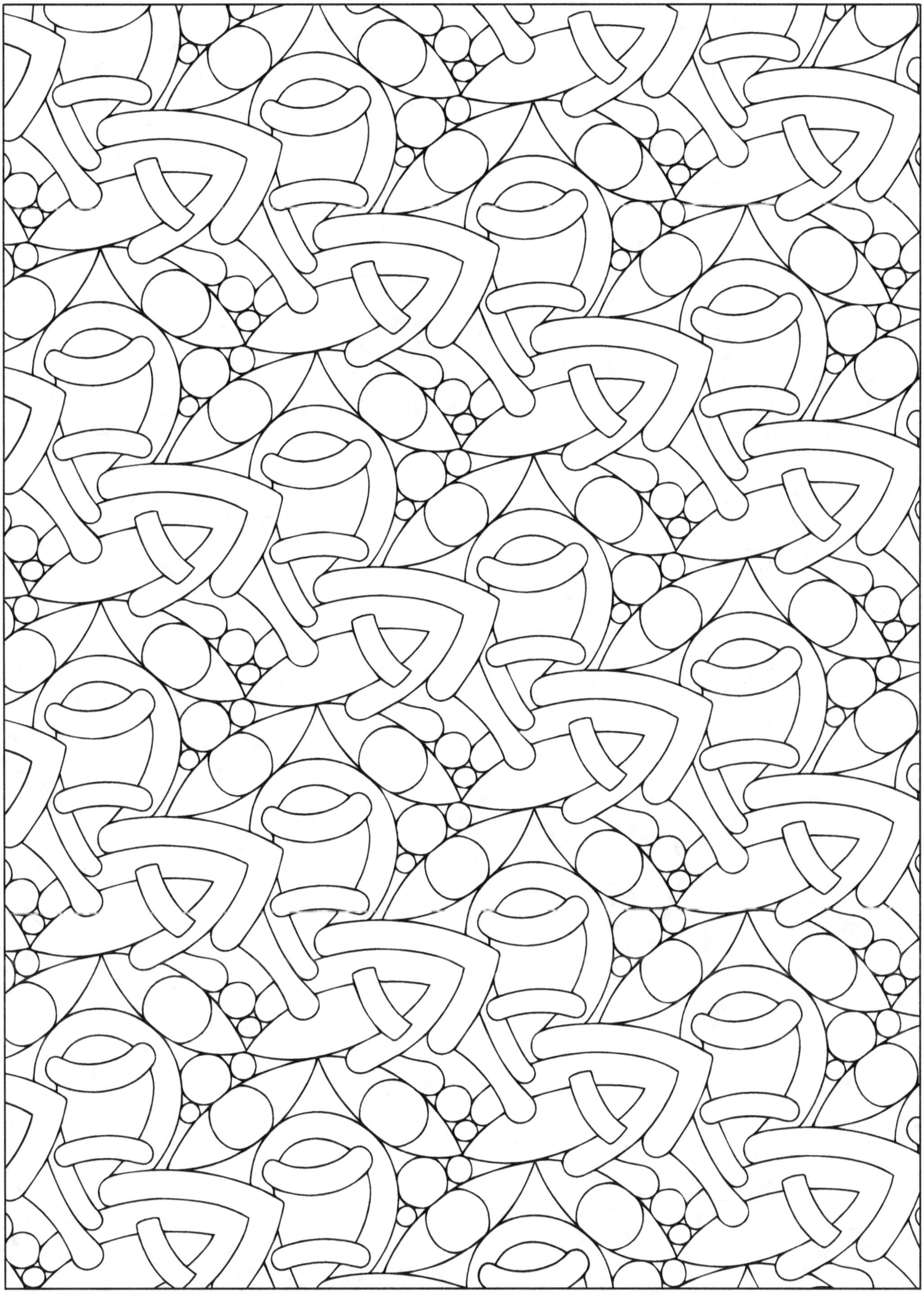

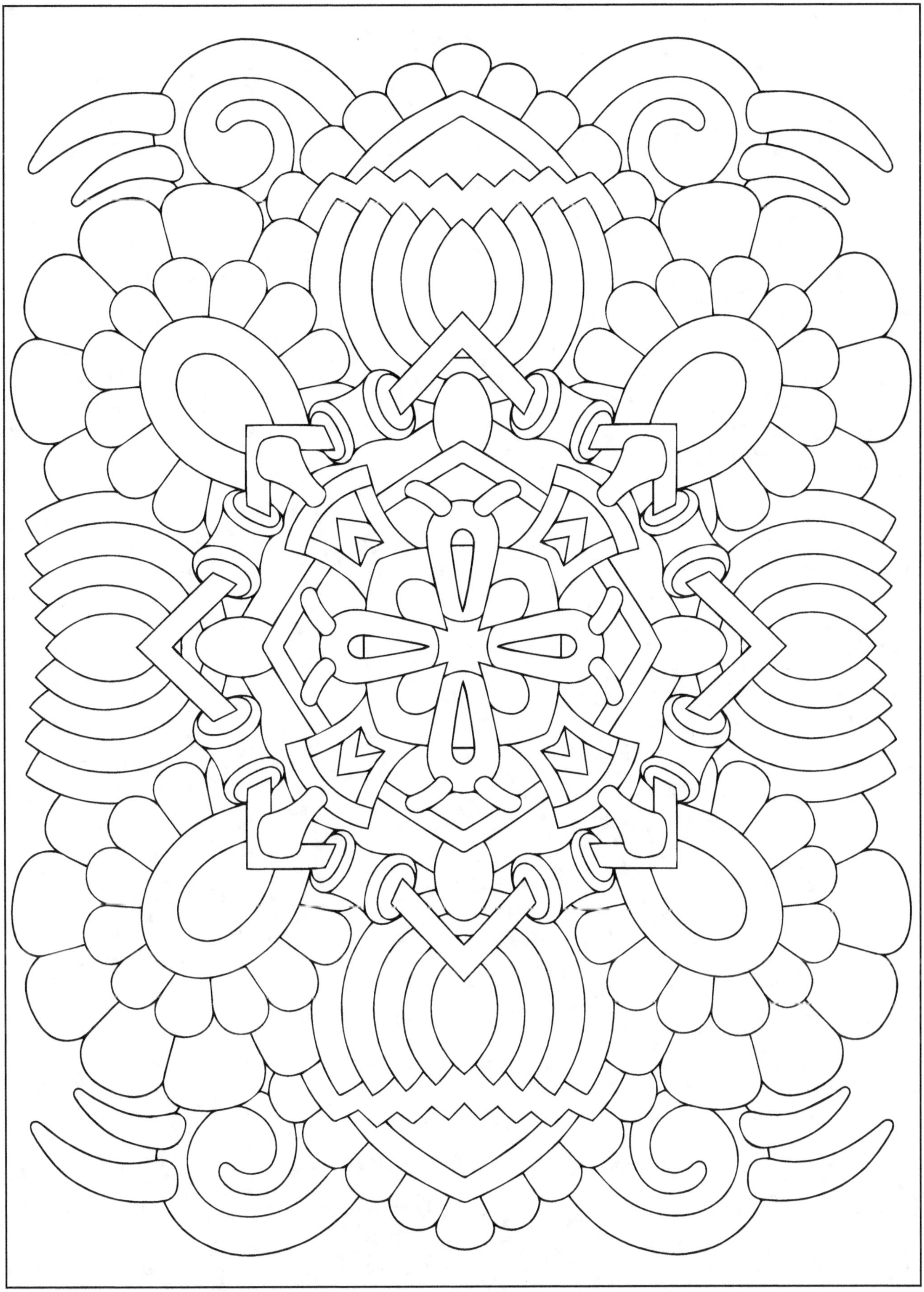

Also by Lori Greenberg

Mandala Coloring Books
Meditative Mandalas - Volume 1
Relaxing Mandalas - Volume 2
Calming Mandalas - Volume 3
Fanciful Mandalas - Volume 4

Pattern Coloring Books
Meditative Patterns - Volume 1
Relaxing Patterns - Volume 2
Calming Patterns - Volume 3

Affirmation Coloring Books
Meditative Affirmations - Volume 1

Find these, and future books on Amazon

Visit **www.lorigreenberg.com**
and join Lori Greenberg's Coloring Connection
Facebook group
for free coloring pages
and updates on new books.

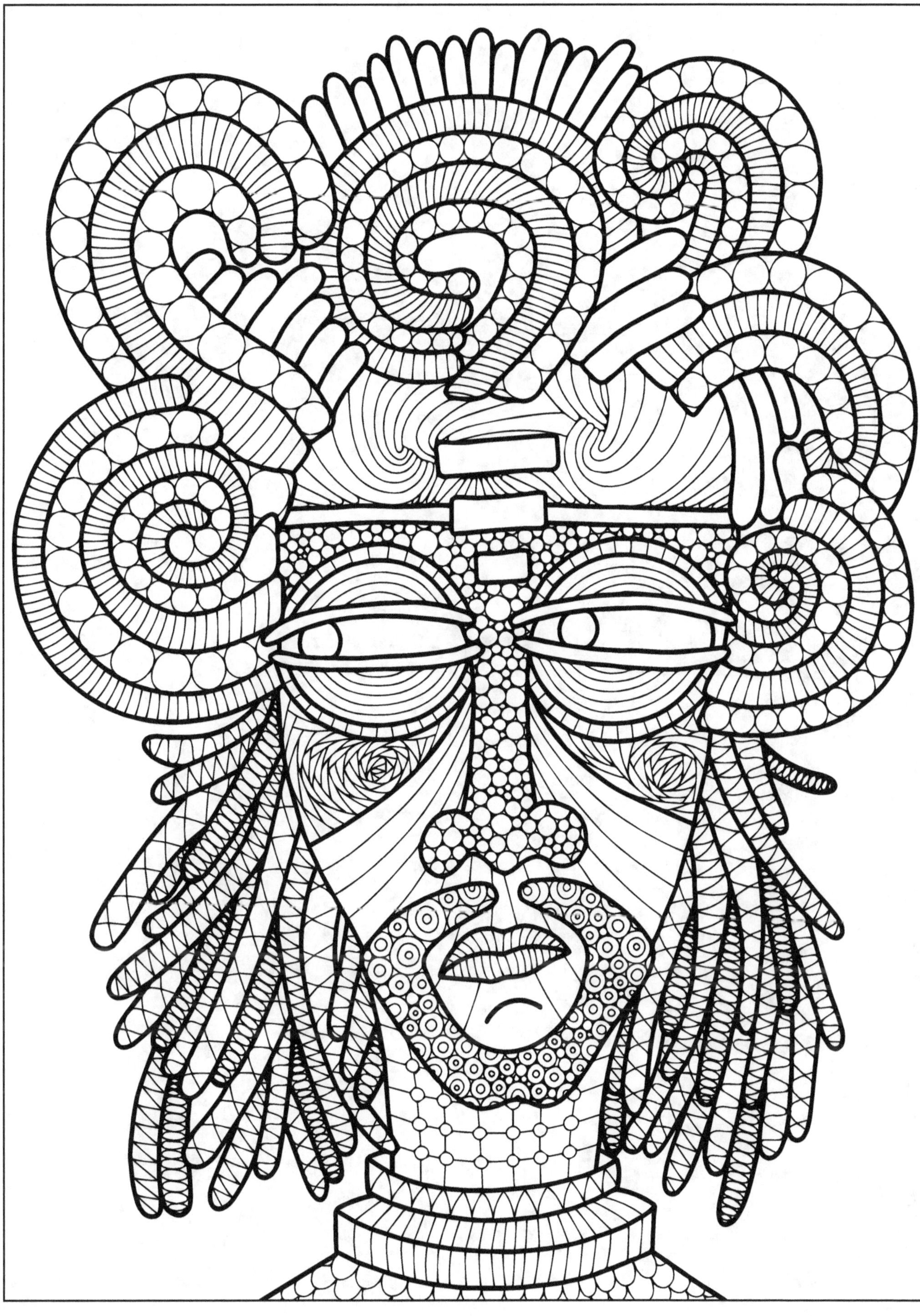

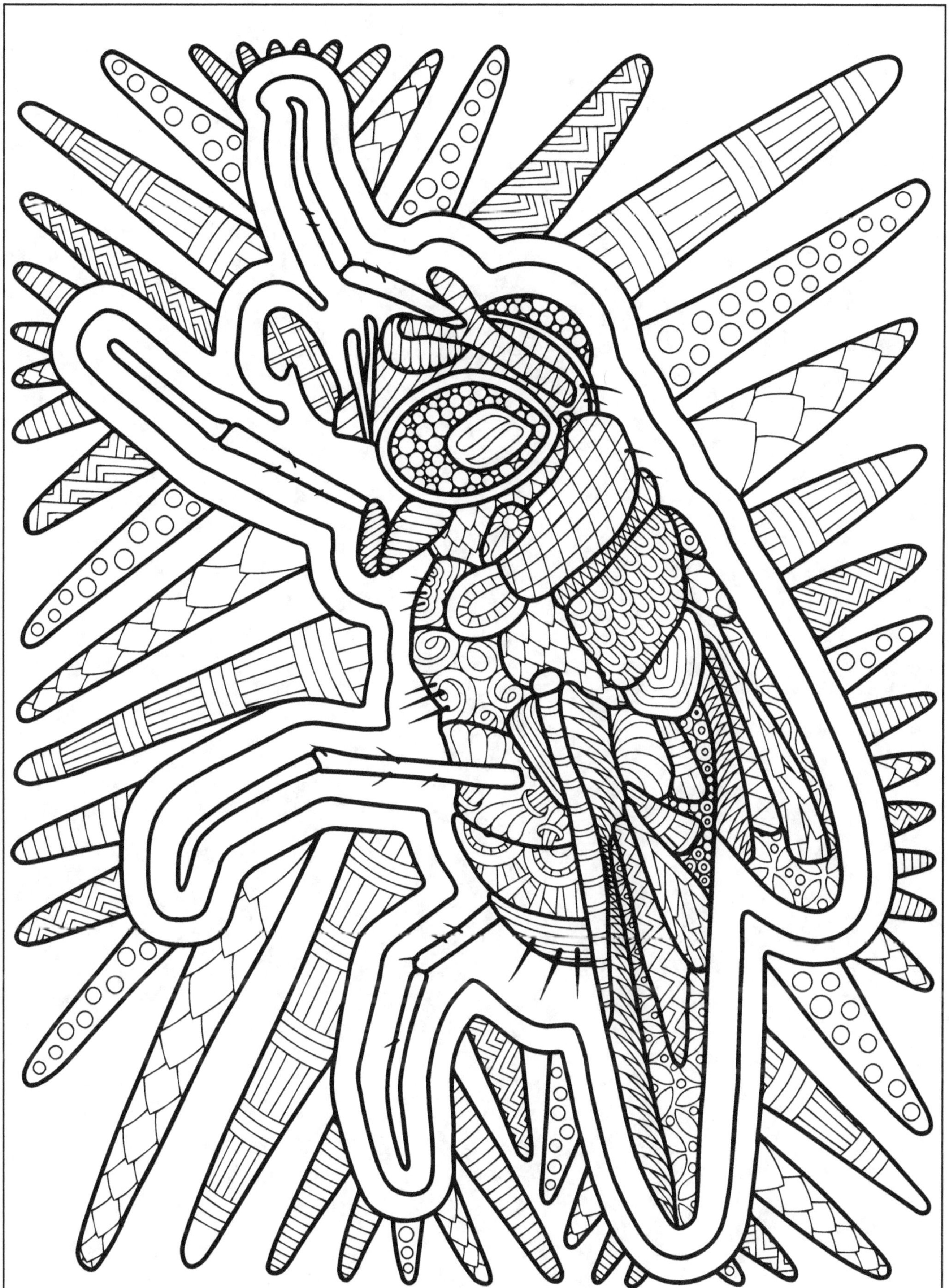

www.ingramcontent.com/pod-product-compliance
Lightning Source LLC
Chambersburg PA
CBHW081138170526
45165CB00008B/2722
* 9 7 8 1 5 4 8 0 5 2 7 7 5 *